WILD FIERCE LIFE

Caitlin Press Inc.
8100 Alderwood Road,
Halfmoon Bay, BC V0N 1Y1
www.caitlin-press.com

Text and cover design by Vici Johnstone
Cover image Sander Jain
Printed in Canada

Caitlin Press Inc. acknowledges financial support from the Government
of Canada and the Canada Council for the Arts, and the Province of
British Columbia through the British Columbia Arts Council and the
Book Publisher's Tax Credit.

Library and Archives Canada Cataloguing in Publication
Streetly, Joanna, author
        Wild fierce life: dangerous moments on the outer coast/ Joanna
Streetly.

ISBN 978-1-987915-65-5 (softcover)
        1. Streetly, Joanna. 2. Authors, Canadian—21st century—Biogra-
phy. 3. Outdoor life—British Columbia—Vancouver Island—Biography.
4. Autobiographies. I. Title.

PS8637.T746Z46 2018   C813'.6   C2017-906531-9

WILD
FIERCE
LIFE

DANGEROUS MOMENTS ON THE OUTER COAST

Joanna Streetly

CAITLIN PRESS

With respect for my Nuu-chah-nulth friends and family, whose friendship and welcome to their territories have made the last thirty years both meaningful and possible.

Contents

PROLOGUE 9

THE BRIGHTNESS AND DARKNESS OF LUCIFER 11

FLIGHT INSTINCT 17

LOSING POWER 31

GHOST CAT 43

SCARS 55

RADIO WAVE 65

ONE BRIGHT STAR 77

BALANCING ACT 87

WILD LIFE 99

BREATHLESS 109

THE COLOUR OF TIME 119

FAIR GAME 125

LETTING GO 137

SAY THE NAMES 151

FINDERS KEEPERS 161

EPILOGUE 173

ACKNOWLEDGEMENTS 174

NOTES 176

Prologue

I was nineteen when I moved to Tofino. Young in all the obvious ways. It was a time before the technology explosion, when boats were expected to leak, or sink, and boat motors were expected to be fickle. It was an era uncomplicated by cellphones or GPS—or even wealth—when simply having a compass elevated me above those who approached the fog with mumbled prayers, or fingers crossed. It was a place where there was a roaring trade in tarps and candles and lamp oil. And it was a place where a good story was valued above all else.

I didn't embark on my new life with any firm plan; rather, at every turn I took the path of least resistance. I found myself drawn to the lands and the waters and the people, and allowed myself to be led further and further in.

I'm not a doyenne of kayaking, or a boater of great renown. I haven't hiked the highest peaks, or crossed the Pacific in perilously small craft. I don't think my resilience equals that of women who've gone before me, raising huge families far from help, with few resources.

But there have been times in wild places when things simply became precarious. And when they did, the intensity of those moments opened previously uncharted regions of myself. I found and lost fears, contemplated death, expanded my understanding of humankind, and of history. I felt time telescope from milliseconds to millennia. And I noted points of inexplicable connection between myself and my surroundings. It is these moments, combined with the jeopardy of their situations, that I've set out to explore and share.

To my parents, whose extraordinary life stories are remembered by many a rapt listener; to Frank Harper of Island Beach, who could tease out the humour, the irony and the synchronicities of any story; and to all those with dangerous moments of their own to tell of—I raise a toast.

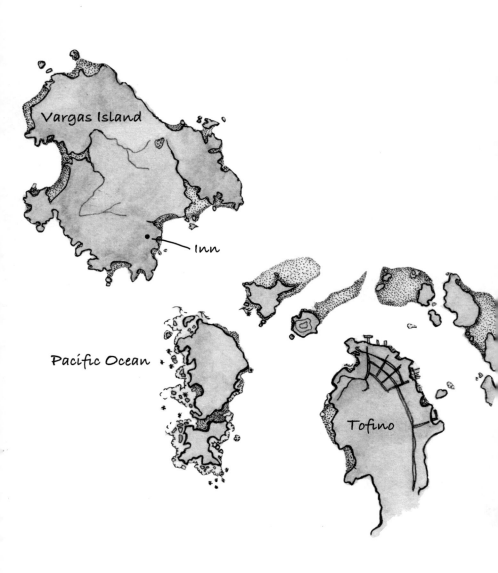

like seed pearls moon-spilt
beads of light skitter and dance
lead me to the deep

The Brightness and Darkness of Lucifer

It was after midnight when I found myself in trouble. My solitude, so eagerly sought, now put me in peril in a way I hadn't foreseen. Earlier, when I'd pulled open the heavy wooden door of the beach sauna, I'd been looking for refuge. I'd peered into the darkened space, heady with the scent of hot cedar planks. Everyone had gone to bed. I slipped inside.

There is always a moment when a role becomes a burden. For outdoor guides, that moment comes with exhaustion, usually at day's end. Until then, every minute has been spent helping others. Even when guests have retired for the night, the guide is preparing for the next day. I'd been up since 5:30 that morning, loading kayaks, giving instruction to my group of six novice kayakers—aging professionals who had chosen beds over Therm-a-Rests—cooking, cleaning up, entertaining, as well as paddling from Tofino—on the west coast of Vancouver Island—to the Vargas Island Inn in Clayoquot Sound. And now the beach sauna's heat offered pleasure; its quiet darkness offered sanctuary. Leaning against the worn hand-milled boards, I was lulled by the sea as it washed the pebbles of the nearby beach. *Hush*, it soothed, even as I fretted over the safety of the kayaks. Yes, I had secured the boats. Yes, the gear was out of the tide's reach.

Hush.

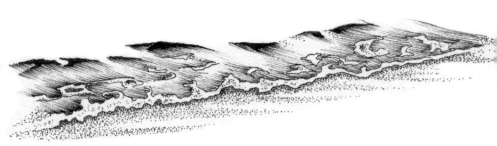

Moisture pearled on my breasts and arms as heat soared outward from the wood stove. I closed my eyes and imagined the fern-laden Sitka spruce towering above my head. The sauna shack was perched above tideline in a curved bay, ringed with old-growth rainforest. After supper, walking to the end of the beach, I'd looked up at the wall of trees, feeling their astonishing mass. Against them, the silhouettes of campfire folk shrank, almost to their vanishing point.

The tide of my day ebbed through my pores. Droplets became a sea, my skin swept with the purging of sweat. Eventually, I peeled myself from the grain of the wood and heaved the door open, giddy with the first breath of cold air. Now for the cold water immersion. No hesitation. The beam of my flashlight guided me as I ran, tender-footed, over pebbles. There was no moon and I felt the water's edge before seeing it. Putting down my flashlight with my towel, I positioned it as a beacon, to guide me back to shore. My eyes closed tight as my head went under.

When I surfaced, gasping and blinking at the viscous salt of sea and sweat, I noticed the haziness of my light. The yellow beam was diffuse. I looked around. In the blackness, I made out the pale opacity of a sea mist. I riffled a hand through the water, wondering what it meant. Would tomorrow's trip be offset by a cold swaddle of mist? Or would the fog vanish the way it had come, in sly increments, slinking from the sun? My musings were interrupted by a flash of brightness:

green light, erupting from my fingertips. Bioluminescence—the stuff of myth and magic.

On the west coast, bioluminescence is usually only seen when the water is at its warmest, in late summer or early fall. It's a chemical light, like that of Will-o-the-wisp's—the mischievous elf of English folklore, whose candle leads the innocent into bogs, or to the cliff's edge. Like undersea fireflies, tiny plankton produce glowing sparks as their internal chemicals react to being disturbed. Just by moving, I could make light—uncommon, miraculous, cold light.

Sinking deeper in the water, I trailed my arm outward, watching the lines of it flicker to life. I stirred the ocean with both arms, appointing myself choreographer of the miracle brightness. Glowing white-green beads strung together in ribbons, flaring and dying as they moved through the black water. A new universe opened itself to me as I swirled and swam—enchanted. Over there, a detonation of flashes; over here, a constellation, the exact shape of my hand; down below, a dark space arrowing up between my lambent, open legs.

Yes, Will-o-the-wisp tricked me, distracted me, pulled me out to sea, deeper than my feet could touch. Unconcerned by the cold water, I twisted and twirled. And when I looked around, I had eyes only for the brilliant mating of two chemicals—luciferin and luciferase. Lucifer, from the Latin, *lucem ferre*, bearer of light; Lucifer, the morning star, now named Venus. Lucifer, another name for Satan.

How long was I distracted? Minutes? Seconds? How to measure timeless moments? A sudden chill shook me from my delight. I looked for the beacon. It wasn't there. My beacon was invisible and so was the shoreline. Fog and darkness were all I could see. But I couldn't be far from shore, could I? I would see it soon. I waited, searching. I waited longer, searching harder. I saw only blackness. This couldn't be happening... I—

I was lost at sea, mere lengths from the beach. Alone, in cold Pacific water, on a remote island, I was shrouded in fog and darkness, unsure which way to swim, my life depending on the right choice. I sharpened my vision, eyes straining, body now hard with fear. Surely the trees would save me and the looming shadow of them would rise above the mist?

I saw nothing.

I pictured something I *could* see. A memory of the tide table, its columns of numbers marking the days, this day's date circled in pencil. Ebbing, the tide would be ebbing. With every tight breath I was being drawn out to sea. I thought of the sleeping guests, tired from their long day and too far away to hear me. I thought of them waking next morning to my disappearance. My legs kicked harder as I treaded water, oblivious to the bioluminescence, turning myself in circles. I didn't dare swim. What if I swam the wrong way?

I listened for waves on the beach, but I heard only the ripple of my own hands as they palmed the surface. I lifted my nose, longing for a trace of campfire smoke, but I smelled only the wetness of salt. I lifted my arms pole-straight above my head and sank, exhaling bubbles and reaching for the bottom with my feet. But I felt only the inky water that surrounded me. In the darkness, I began to function on two levels at once. Survival instincts guided my body while thoughts blossomed in my mind.

Like many people, I'd heard that those faced with death would see their lives pass in front of their eyes. But my life lay within me, tidy and complete—peaceful. In that moment, it didn't matter if life ended now, or later. All moments became one moment, distilled into a single sensation. Why was I taught to fight death, I wondered, when instead there could be this sense of perfection? Death's beautiful secret lay before me, tantalizingly unexplored. But my father had always taught me to fight. I'd grown up with tales of his escapes from snakes, sharks, deep jungles, Himalayan peaks. Failure to survive would be just that—failure. My father had been a meteor, streaking the bright sky of my young life. How would he judge me for "giving in" to death after an error in judgment? How would society judge me? In my brush with Lucifer, would people see the brightness of Venus, or the darkness of Satan? Might my private moment of perfection be declared a tragedy?

The inviolable nature of my death-secret perplexed me. I would want others to know that I'd died well. And yet, I could see the allure of a gift so personal that it could be felt by no one but me. I thought again of my parents, wondering at their own death-secrets. A sense of potential swelled within me, instead of grief. Then my palm brushed something soft and my thoughts vanished.

I gasped and turned, kicking hard. The motion of my feet disturbed more plankton and there, in front of me, was a long piece of bull kelp, *Nereocystis luetkeana*, ignited into whiteness, lit to perfection. I watched the graceful blades streaming silver in the current. I saw them reaching away from me, finning and sparkling as the water rippled the length of them and hurried on out to sea. I saw my body sliding toward them, being carried the same way.

A small clue, but my only clue. I faced myself away from the blades of kelp. Away from the open sea they pointed toward. I made my choice.

And I swam.

As I swam, my eyes refocused on an imagined shoreline. I barely breathed, longing for the beacon to appear. I swam with confidence and doubt slamming together within me. I swam with the brightness and darkness of Lucifer. I swam with a secret within me. I swam until my feet grazed the bottom and I heard the hush of water smoothing pebbles.

Hush.

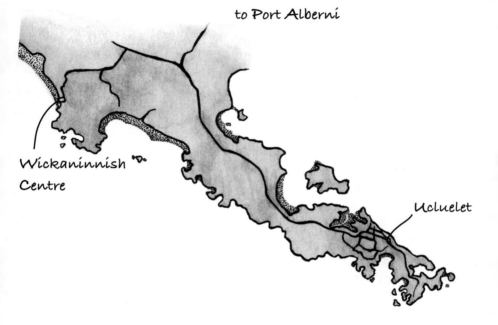

*the sky walks with me
silvering wet sand. My feet
splash through cloud puddles*

Flight Instinct

When I was a girl in Trinidad, I learned to draw seabirds with two simple curved lines—a loose m. The curves adorned my childscapes: cloudless sky, turquoise water and sandy beach marked only by a perfect line of footprints. The footprints were copied from countless postcard images selling the allure of solitude. Seabirds took the idea a little further, soaring away from Earth—free.

As a young teen at school in England, I was well versed in the notion of solitude. *The Secret Garden, Jane Eyre, Wuthering Heights*—I read them all, picturing lonely moors as I looked out over farm fields from the windows of my grandmother's large, empty house. In choir, I sang a musical arrangement of "I wandered lonely as a cloud," Wordsworth's daffodil poem, in which he rhapsodizes over "the bliss of solitude." Later still, I discovered *Wind, Sand and Stars* by Antoine de Saint-Exupéry, a writer whose lyrical flow of words was often inspired by being "alone with the vast tribunal that is the stormy sky." Saint-Exupéry's love for the sky was infectious. But only now, as an adult, have I comprehended the depth of his experiences. Immersed as I was in youth and swept by his obvious passion, I never fully understood that his carefully constructed teachings were learned through harsh experience. I adored his classic children's novella *The Little Prince,* but I perceived it solely as a thing of beauty, not as I see it now: a cautionary tale.

I'm standing on the suspension bridge platform. Below me, Lynn Canyon is a veritable snake pit, seething with November floodwater. A continuous wall of white-brown froth charges over the lip of the cliff and explodes downward into the mess of the canyon. The sheer rock walls transmit the energy upward, causing the bridge cables to swing, creak, vibrate. Every year there are deaths here—girls and boys of summer, jumping from the cliffs into drought-stricken, too-shallow pools, or being held underwater by the downward force of the currents. I understand the thrill, but I also see the way peer pressure changes the equation. I'm eighteen and I'm on my daily mountain-bike commute to Capilano University in North Vancouver. It's early in the morning and there's no one around to peer pressure me, so I do it myself. It's taken months for me to gain confidence at this. But now I pull the bike between my legs and point it at the narrow bridge. Who needs coffee, when they can have a shot of adrenaline? If the bike throws me, I might tumble over the safety cables, into the canyon. *If.* I breathe the word "go" and swoop across the narrow swaying bridge, picking up speed on the descent and slowing again as I near the platform on the far side.

Propelled by exhilaration, I fly up the trail, even though my tires are bogged down on the steep wet path. Cedar and hemlock trees block out the already dim light of the shortening days. By December, I will be using a headlamp to get through the forest in the mornings. In January, who knows what I'll be doing? That's when my practicum work placement is due to start. And so far I've failed to arrange anything. I've chosen the field of nature interpretation, but my foreign student visa prohibits me from working for money. It's complicated, stressful. Somewhere in the tangle lies the viability of a life in Canada. I emerge from the darkness onto the Seymour Demonstration Forest road. From here, it's all downhill. But instead of coasting, I urge the bike onward. Today is the day I find out if Pacific Rim National

Park will accept me as an international student volunteer. If they do, my practicum dilemma will be over. I fly downhill into the campus, screeching to a halt at our department's small free-standing building, where my friends are gathered. "Joey!" calls Kristy—a laughing, white-blonde girl, possibly the friendliest person I've ever met. The way she greets people, you'd think she hasn't seen them since last year. Her vivacity is infectious. I smile back and greet my friends.

Pacific Rim National Park. I can't believe my luck! I've been longing to find a way back to the west coast of Vancouver Island ever since a two-week kayaking trip in Kyuquot Sound when I was seventeen. The trip was life altering, causing me to abandon my reluctant plan to study English literature at Birmingham University. On our logging-road route back to civilization after the trip, I stood outside a diner in a tiny town called White River and swore—with the absolute conviction of youth—that I would never darken the doors of an office block, or windowless workspace. My transition to a career in Outdoor Recreation may have seemed sudden to some, but right then outside that diner, in air thick with french fry grease, it made perfect sense to me.

At school I most enjoy the outdoor skills programs, love the earth sciences—ecology, geology, climatology—and yawn a little over topics such as special event planning and business management. It is my inspiring science teacher who has arranged for me to study west coast natural history and nature interpretation at the Wickaninnish Interpretive Centre, in the Long Beach unit of the park. The Centre is fifteen kilometres from Ucluelet, not an impossible biking distance despite the steep hills involved. As it is winter, I will have the beach, and the Centre, mostly to myself. The Pacific might not be turquoise at this latitude, but that line of postcard-perfect footprints will lead to me.

It's the beginning of a new year; I'm peering through misted-up bus windows at the dark, rain-wet road unspooling through the endless forest. My stuffed-full expedition backpack and beloved mountain bike wait for me under the bus like loyal talismans. I've shared many adventures with both of them and I know they make good companions. Eventually, a strand of roadside buildings appears, loosely strung from one end of the town to the other. The bus makes several stops, dropping off bundles of newspapers. There is no bus station and it takes me a while to realize when it's time to get out.

My first night, I roam the eightplex compound where I've been assigned free housing. It's mid-winter and no one else is living here. The units sit dark and empty like so many caves, waiting to be filled by summer-season staff. Something about the emptiness makes me shiver. Perhaps it's the echo. The compound is recessed from the road in a treed area, set around a central parking lot. On one side of my unit, a tangle of trees and undergrowth is within touching distance; on the other, security lights from the parking area flood the small kitchen window. Turn one way and the forest welcomes me; turn the other way and I might be in jail.

I wake to a neighbourhood cat, curled on a round cushion of dense orange moss in a tree outside my window. The cushion is a perfect fit and provides the cat with a lookout spot, fifteen feet above the forest floor. I imagine the cat's body heat and rumbling purr being absorbed by the moss. I warm my hands on a mug of tea and take in the slow spotlight of its swivelling gaze, the ginger paws pressed against its heart. The warmth and contentment of the cat seem like a good omen, facing me in the right direction.

Ucluelet is a company town in thrall to MacMillan Bloedel, the multinational company dominating the coastal logging industry. There is a visible pickup-truck fraternity, and company loyalty is fierce. Environmentalists are a direct threat. M&B, as they are known, have carried out the clear-cutting of Mount Ozzard, which rises up on the north side of the Ucluelet Harbour, and which Ucluelet townsfolk look at daily as part of their view, low cloud permitting. If I, or M&B, were to become skilled at reading tea leaves, we might foresee the demise of M&B in three years' time, during the Clayoquot Sound protests of 1993. But I'm brand new on the coast—a greenhorn. And as a bike-riding, backpack-toting student, working at the park—as far as the fraternity is concerned, I have Environmentalist written all over me.

My place of work, the Wickaninnish Centre, doesn't disappoint. It's situated on a rocky point with the beach wrapped around it and the high tide sweeping against its foundations. I imagine the rumble of Pacific storms, my face pressed against wave-dashed windows. There is even an ocean observation room upstairs, with cushioned window seats for just that purpose. The main part of the building—a dim, barn-like space—is painted with a massive mural of the gloomy offshore depths, dominated by a large humpback whale. I am to share an office with the soft-spoken woman who will oversee my learning when she is not in the field or away at meetings. My desk faces the wall, but a small window on my right looks out onto the log-strewn terminus of Wickaninnish Beach. That first lunch break, my supervisor and I walk the beach to the sand dunes, where she shows me a uniquely shifting world, set back from the high-tide zone, dotted with small islands of stunted trees. The following day we walk over to South Beach, where Pacific swells crash onto rocky stacks, exploding into white foam. Every few seconds the beach changes colour, from frothy white to steel grey, as heavy waves pound the dark sand, rushing up the steep incline before being sucked back into the roiling mess of the bay. A mist hangs over the stacks, like the ghosts of so many waves. I breathe in the spray, exhilaration flooding my lungs. I can't think of anywhere I'd rather be.

In my practicum days, there is no email, no Internet. Social media is not simply a screen away. I connect with my family in England only by international mail. Calling my friends in Vancouver will require a visit to the bank for the pound-weight of quarters I'll need to feed the pay phone. At the eightplex, if I want to connect with other people, I'll have to go into town and introduce myself—label and all. It's January. I rise in darkness, hauling on cycling gear as the wind whips rain and tree branches against my bedroom wall. I clip a bike helmet over my rainproof hood and stash lunch and dry clothes in my backpack. The first few kilometres of the road are lit with street lights. Then the true darkness begins. The shoulder is narrow and several of the hills are long and steep. The road undulates and snakes, up and down, side to side. My light picks out the white line and I follow it, surprised when my front wheel drops into a deep pothole and slaps muddy water across my face. One hill in particular is long, the ascent sustained. I breathe hard, looking down at the asphalt, not up at the hilltop. It may be an optical illusion, but when I can't see the incline, the biking seems easier.

A beam of light illuminates my way-finding and I'm distracted by the passage of a car. By the time I make out the park decal, it's already passed me. Still… a fellow park worker! Solidarity surges through me. Then another car passes. And another. A stream, all with a single driver, all representing Environment Canada. They zoom by as if I'm invisible, their lights disappearing into the future, leaving me suddenly blind in the darkness. The feeling of solidarity wanes, but returns a few minutes later when another truck passes, this one full of workers. As it, too, disappears ahead of me, I realize that it is a crummy, the nickname given to the white, cube-shaped forest-worker transport vehicles. Environmentalists and loggers—everyone is going to work, bees to their prescribed flowers.

When I reach the Millstream subdivision, a glow lights the glimpse of inlet water. Behind me the grey dawn is striving for effect, throwing washes of shadow over the receding mountains. It's a good place to pause, about a third of the way there, but the biggest of the hills has been conquered. Later, after fifty minutes of steady biking in light that ranges from dark to dim, I freewheel down a short, steep stretch of road to the Centre, where I wander through the cavernous dark space to my office. My supervisor sets me up with reading material and retreats to her computer, arranging her day before leaving for a meeting. At lunchtime, I walk the beach, marvelling at the onslaught of the weather, the relentless shoreward thrust of the ocean. And as the day comes to a close, I pull on my cycling gear and start the journey home, arriving—as I left—in darkness.

At the eightplex, with lights to banish the darkness, I prepare supper and read a book. There is no radio and no TV. I consider listening to music on my Walkman, but batteries are a luxury, so I set a limit. Side A or side B, not both. I choose Creedence Clearwater Revival for the sing-along value—a warm reminder of happy hiking trips. I wonder if the cat is still on his cushion of moss, but it's too dark to tell. As my head touches the pillow I make a note of the deep, splashy pothole and remind myself to avoid it tomorrow.

As a child, I wandered the many empty rooms of my grandmother's house when I was sent there for month-long holidays. Exploring the unpeopled, unlit Wickaninnish Centre doesn't seem much different from those wanderings. Technically, I'm used to being by myself. Likewise, walking the beach alone doesn't seem much different than walking the English countryside for hours when I was a teenager. The only challenge of my new situation seems to be the graveyard feel of the eightplex. There is an eeriness to the way the parking area lights flicker over my sleeping eyes and the tree branches brush against the walls of my room. As the weeks pass, these little things, combined with the never-ending storms and rain, begin to bother me. The lack of daylight—exacerbated by the relentless low-pressure systems and pouring rain—is a constant obstacle. There is something textural about the winter darkness in the rainforest, as if it is a living being—a power-hungry tyrant seeking to expand its empire. Even when the wind and the rain are absent, the darkness presses in on me, an unwanted, ever-present companion.

Two nights a week I have aerobics to look forward to. I've signed up for the social contact and struggle through the routines, never improving, hopelessly unable to mimic the instructor. But other than my supervisor, the leotarded ladies at aerobics vanish when the class is over. In Ucluelet, only the cashier at the Co-op calls me by my name. Her badge says *Joanne*, so I'd pointed out that we were almost name-sisters. Perhaps I should introduce myself to people more often. Weekends seem to last forever. I read books, play the flute, walk, ride my bike, stock up on groceries, read more books. Time takes on a warped quality, unpredictable in its speed of passage. Once or twice the cat returns to the cushion of moss, bringing its state of contentment with it. I imagine its smooth ginger head rubbing against my ankles, the arch of its back under my hand. I imagine having a warm companion as I read my book on the couch. Sometimes I open the door, to see if it is there. It never is. Instead, as isolation grows around me, I go more frequently to the cashier's till at the Co-op for that one moment of recognition.

Without social contact, I have only my imagination for company. I'm reading *Anna Karenina* and my mind is papered with the complex twists and turns of the plot. My thoughts become demanding, crying out for resolution. They mingle with casual observations that come about as I navigate my surroundings—the raven on my morning doorstep, would Anna consider it an omen? Should I? On lunchtime walks, I often find myself seated on a log, unable to continue walking because I need to finish thinking.

I'm riding to work. I've navigated the pothole and tackled the steepest hill in record time. The Parks Canada vehicles have passed me, one by one, their sightless occupants reminding me of people in dreams, the ones you need help from but who can't seem to hear you.

I stop for the sunrise at Millstream, gold on grey. The crummy passes me, *late*, I think to myself.

But as it passes something moves in the window of the rear door. It is a hand. Someone is waving at me. The moment is so brief, I could be mistaken. The hand forms an image in my mind's eye, surrounded by the negative space of the window. Pale hand, dark window. The centreline of the road is transposed onto the image, like the lifeline of the hand. My heart is in that hand. *Lines of the heart, lines in the land, centre lines, railway lines, Anna Karenina throwing herself under a train, omens, omens, a raven knifing overhead, black and fast.* At the turnoff to Wickaninnish Road, a red-tailed hawk plummets from a tree into the grassy verge, startling me. I stop my bicycle and watch the scimitar beak stabbing and plucking at a small furred mouse or vole. I marvel at the ruffled plumage of the bird, its disregard of me, its bloodlust. Hunger.

It's lunchtime. I'm walking the beach alone, as usual. I sit on a log, wishing Anna Karenina could choose a better way, gazing at the sand, not really seeing it. Then a picture forms, bright and vivid, of a cut running lengthwise along the artery of a pale bare wrist. It is about two inches long, deeply incised and freshly done. Bright drops of blood bubble to the edges, ready to spring from the wound. The cut isn't real. I know that. But the wrist is. I recognize it. It's mine.

I leap up and look around to see if anyone else is on the beach. Even the sight of another person might help dispel the picture. But the beach is empty. I walk back to work, hoping my supervisor will be in the office. Once I see that she is at her desk, I take up my pen and continue the illustration of a Brandt's cormorant I'm working on. It doesn't matter that there is quietness, what matters is her presence. I quickly forget the wrist image and wrap up the day with the drawing accomplished.

That night, however, I'm just getting into bed when the image recurs. It's just as vivid and my throat tightens. I try to shrug it off, but somehow it persists, lingering the way a bad dream can linger even after waking. I divert myself by reading, but I'm still reading at three in the morning, reluctant to turn off the light. The next day I ride my bike to work in a state of wide-awake tiredness. The image presents itself several times that day. Always, I push it away.

Not only does the wrist image recur with increasing frequency, it interrupts my thoughts. No longer can I follow a thought to completion. My mind is peppered with this ghoulish message. Why? I like my life. I don't want to cut my wrist and I don't want anyone else to, either. I don't want to think about the image, but I constantly find myself doing so. I want to sleep at night, but I'm unable to let go, scared of what the image might do to me while I'm sleeping. The storms continue; the rain seldom lets up. I walk around the empty Wickaninnish Centre during the day and I pace the empty eightplex at night. Some mornings I shake with exhaustion. I begin to "miss" sections of my bicycle commute. I suddenly wonder how I've come to reach the junction, or the turnoff. I have no memory of long stretches of the journey.

One day at work, I see The Wrist more times than I can count. My weary eyelids close—*blink*—and there is the image. I wonder if it's now burned into my retinas, like the sun when I've seen it with my naked eyes. To distract myself I walk around the Centre, faster and faster, until I'm almost jogging. The jogging helps, but as soon as I slow down—*blink*—there's The Wrist, superimposed upon the gloomy depths of the deep-sea mural. *Blink*—there it is hovering in front of the life-sized Nuu-chah-nulth whaling canoe. No matter where I go, the image comes with me. My lunch goes uneaten. I barely drink water. I flee home on my bike, cycling faster than ever before, trying to out-race myself. At home I collapse, the image flickering through my brain like a shorting-out fluorescent tube.

Unable to eat, or sleep, I go to the Co-op and exchange precious bills for a stack of quarters. There's a tinkling waterfall of sound as the coins pour into the pay phone and I call Kristy. "Joey!" she exclaims in her always-happy voice, "your ears must be burning! There's a gang of us here and we were just wondering how things are going for you?" She clamps a hand over the receiver and yells, "Guess what, you guys—it's Joanna!!" A distant chorus of shouts reaches my ears, variations on the theme of *Hi, how're you doing?* My legs begin to tremble and I slide down the wall, laughing and shaking. Dimly, I realize that I can't remember the last time I've laughed. The phone is passed from person to person. I talk and laugh and talk some more, using up every last quarter. In all that time I never once see The Wrist. A welcome breeze blows through me. "Can I come and visit you next weekend?" I blurt as I'm saying goodbye. "For sure!" says Kristy, her voice distorted by the beep as the money runs out. I sit on the floor, holding the receiver as if it's a new talisman in my life. What would Anna Karenina think of that?

It's ridiculous, of course. I can't afford the bus fare. But my flight instinct has kicked in. I request time off, borrow money and leave on a Friday, arriving in North Vancouver late that night. Warmth and noise radiate from my friend's small ground-floor apartment, which is packed with familiar faces. I dive into the melee, whooping as I hug one friend after another. Even the music blaring from a ghetto blaster is something to celebrate. My life has been so quiet! I down a can of beer in three gulps and feel the alcohol run through me. In this moment, I am invulnerable. The Wrist can't find me here. I could be dreaming, but I don't care. I waltz into the living room and begin a charade. Comedy. The role of me at aerobics classes.

That Sunday I make my way back to the coast, not knowing what I will face on my return. I know only one thing: if I can't live by myself, life is going to be messy. Whatever my situation, I'll have to get on with it. In fact, the week after I return, a park employee arrives for the season, moving into the unit next to mine. The following week I'm invited to Friday night volleyball in Tofino—fun games followed by a visit to the pub. My days no longer begin and end in darkness. At work, interpreters arrive, abuzz with stories of how they've spent their winters. And that's how I realize that winter is over. The daylight has returned, changing everything.

❧

Studies involving isolation and solitary confinement show that sleep disruptions and hallucinations are common. Often the participants become so distressed they cannot continue with the study and ask to be released. Prisoners are not so lucky. Such conditions are more extreme than mine were. And yet the lack of daylight and human connection obviously took their toll on me. Only much later did I begin to see things from a distance. I pieced together the days and the nights, wondered how many times a day I may have spoken, or been spoken to, considered the absence of pets or family members. I factored in the weather, the darkness, the silence, the echoing eightplex.

At the time, though, I didn't think about what had happened. The experience was either present, or absent. And once it was absent,

I forgot it. Like the seabirds of my childhood, my life arrowed off to more and more remote locations. A lack of housing in Tofino was responsible for the collection of islands and floathouses I later came to call home, and my profession as a kayak guide led me often into wilderness. But as a one-time lesson in life—a teachable moment to prepare me for my future—my brush with isolation showed me what a trap it could be.

Antoine de Saint-Exupéry wrote that the only true form of wealth was "that of human contact." He learned about isolation and survival after crashing his radio-less plane in the Sahara Desert in 1935. I didn't have to crash a plane to put myself in his shoes, but nowadays when I read *The Little Prince*, I see one man's elegy to loneliness. And like the Little Prince wondering about his rose, I've tried to go back in time to find the girl I was then, reaching for her in the grey light of my inner eye. But in my meditations she eludes me. There is the soft white glow of bone and two dark eyes. Never a face, never a voice, never a thought. I've seen a capsule of roots, grown dense over the years, and once a glimpse of limbs, bunched and muscular, springing away from me. For all my inner exploration, what sticks with me is a white bird, exploding out and away from the cage of roots, later lodging in my third eye, where the fluttering wings still fan my thoughts.

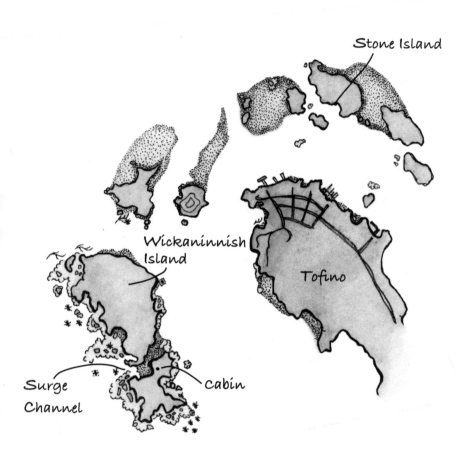

*the outer isles sing
their wave-battered songs, tell tales
of storm wrack and woe*

Losing Power

It's a late-September morning in 1993. I'm drinking a mug of tea, one hand raised against golden, low-slanted sunlight. Airborne mew gulls are feasting on insects, wheeling and crying. Over and over they loop the sky, calling out summer's end in sweet-sad notes—*meeeewww!* From my cabin at Stone Island, I am looking south across the harbour at small, forested islands and glass-like water. I can see Tofino's waterfront, where barely a boat is moving. Nothing in my view hints at the possibility that a mile farther out to sea the morning is not equally peaceful. Or that a surfer at the beach might be enthusing over the unusually large swell, formed by a storm far, far away across the Pacific.

Other than the gulls, little else stirs. If I speak, or move, I could shatter the moment. I'm awake and conscious, but untethered in the hypnotic way that only seems possible at the beginning of a day. Steam rises up from my mug and I hover over it, inhaling, while an invisible tide of thoughts slips in and out of my mind. The quiet is even sweeter than sleep. Later in the morning I will remember this feeling and long to recapture it. But when two squirrels break into a noisy argument and skitter branch to branch in the hemlock tree beside me, I pour the dregs of my tea onto the roots of a yellowing tomato plant and go inside. My day off from work is not a day of freedom.

Marine charts of Clayoquot Sound are like an artist's study in colour values; blues, greens, tan and white. Nowhere is the land uniform. Fjord-like inlets knife their way deeply into mountains, while rocks and islands pockmark every expanse of blue. Some mountains rise and fall with sensual curves, while others are steep and angular, their contour lines packed tight like cards. Shorelines are shown as inky squiggles in steep rocky areas, or green-dotted swaths of mudflat, or wide curves of sand. Some islands are large enough to carry their own mountains, while other islands are only a couple of acres. Still others are mere rocks, proud bearers of a single tree.

This summer, my partner Carl has been building a small cabin on the tiny outer-coast island of Echachis. The island was once a traditional summer whaling village and is a significant part of his Tla-o-qui-aht heritage. Lacking a single contour line, Echachis is represented on the chart as a tan-coloured splot. It is surrounded by blue that quickly becomes the white of the open Pacific. No other land stands between Echachis and Japan. No barriers protect it from storms. This island is the vanguard, its rocky shoreline inked with clusters of reefs and navigational hazards. The roughed-in cabin is about to be boarded up for winter, as the combination of building materials, small boats and heaving seas can be disastrous. The extreme outer coast of the Pacific Northwest presents an elevated quotient of danger. Islands like Echachis may seem like paradise in summertime, but winter storms transform everything.

Although Echachis is visible from Tofino, the cabin is on the far side of the island, facing the sunset. One way to get there is the circuitous, ocean-exposed way, which culminates in a narrow surge channel, barely visible on the chart—the marine equivalent of a one-car alley between buildings—replete with lurking rocks and surf. There is also a direct, sheltered route, which passes between Echachis and Wickaninnish islands over the sandbar that connects them at low tide. Either route involves strict observance of the tides. A retreating tide can beach a boat in seconds, leaving the occupants marooned for up to twelve hours, possibly longer. Always, it is preferable to make the trip with two people: one to hold a shoreline; the other to throw anchors, raise the motor and pass goods overboard.

This golden day offers a chance to retrieve a generator, which I need at Stone Island. The tide should be high enough for me to take the easy route, which is the most important thing. I should have a second person to help me carry the generator, but I brush that problem aside. Asking for help is a personal battlefield. There is the creeping sense of defeat that goes with every request, the feeling that—as a woman—I am not capable. The youngest of five siblings, I was always the last to be chosen for tasks or opportunities. Nowadays, I make up for lost time by choosing myself wherever possible. So today, while I do need help with the generator, I can't face asking for any. I have a hazy plan (90 percent willpower and 10 percent physics) to form loose lumber into railway-style tracks. By some miracle the tracks will also convey the generator from the rocks to the boat... I mentally gloss over that particular detail and chuck a coil of rope into my little open boat. I check the gas tank: half full—more than enough.

On days when the sea is glass calm, driving a boat is akin to flying. I feel as if I'm a bird—a shearwater perhaps—inches from the surface, adjusting my angle of glide, and soaring. Sea and sky blend into a single bright future. There is pleasure in carving a turn and feeling the responsiveness of a boat's hull. There is elation at the rush of air, the speed.

On this morning the boat ride seems to make everything possible. The fallibilities of my plan are eclipsed by the pleasure of the moment and the impossible breadth of the horizon. As I head for Duffin Passage, my eyes are fixed on the faraway blip of land that is Echachis and it's only by chance that I glance over at First Street Dock and see the blur of two arms waving. I recognize Rob, a carpenter who has been helping with the cabin. He's trying to flag me down. It turns out that Rob has just paddled in from Echachis, where he stayed overnight. He wants to return, bringing his tools with him. But his tools won't fit in his nineteen-foot expedition-style sea kayak. He asks for a ride, but he says the tide won't be high enough for us to go the easy way. I look again at the calm harbour and shove the first crate of Rob's tools into the bow of my boat. More crates follow. As my thirteen-foot Boston Whaler transforms into a pint-sized freight barge, I wonder how I'm going to fit Rob and his kayak, too. We strap the kayak on top of the crates, its bow jutting for'ard like a tall-ship's prow. We leave a perfect space for Rob to crouch on the bench right next to me.

My boat has been built with a number of safety features in mind: enough floatation to survive being swamped by waves; a trimaran hull and a low centre of gravity for stability; and low sides, to avoid buffeting by wind. Even though she is so small and close to the water, the boat has proved herself on the ocean time after time. As loaded as she is at this moment, I have faith in her ability to take Rob, his kayak, his tools and me to Echachis. But as we pull away from First Street Dock, I note the slowing effect of all the weight on the boat. It takes us a while to get up onto a plane, even though I nudge the throttle to maximum. The engine roars and eclipses any chance of conversation.

We leave the flat waters of the harbour and head toward a narrow, rocky passage leading to the open ocean. Here, a large swell rolls toward us, crests and breaks. This is so unexpected that I stop the boat while I am still on the safe side of the passage, mentally abandoning the trip. But Rob is blasé. "It's not that bad," he says. "I paddled it this morning." I consider his opinion. Swell can be manageable when the sea surface is smooth and there is a reasonable distance between each wave. Rob is also a sea kayak guide, so his judgment should be reliable.

I wait for the series of waves to pass. Then I gun the motor, ploughing against the added weight and pushing through the passageway. Halfway out to the northwestern tip of Wickaninnish Island, doubt returns and I slow the boat again. But once again Rob reassures me that the outer coast is really not that bad—he says he knows I can do it. I've been driving boats for years, yet his belief in me still feels good. When I first moved to the coast, boating was a primarily male-dominated field. I had to prove my credentials. I consider those credentials now as I go forward at half-throttle. Boat handling skill is the outward marker of ability. Experience and judgment are the invisibles.

When we reach Wickaninnish Island, the outer-coast section of the route comes into view and I see what lies ahead. Everything is moving—heaving and tossing. And everything is white. Silvery sea-foam is being blasted into the air where it catches the morning light. The location of the reefs, usually hidden, is now fully revealed as the swells surge over them and erupt into frothing tiers of brightness. We are only one nautical mile from our destination, but the path will be a minefield of watery explosions. Forget credentials. Without even slowing, I turn the boat around.

"What are you doing?" yells Rob. "You can't go back, we're nearly there!"

I gesture at all his gear and at the ocean. "I'm not doing it; it's not safe," I shout above the roar of surf.

"What do you mean?" he yells back, "You can't turn around now. We'll make it, no problem." Unerringly, he finds my weak point. Perhaps I have somehow led him to it: "And I always thought you were a *real* west coaster," he says.

⁂

I come from a family of risk-takers. Name an improbable situation and my father likely escaped from it. My mother, too, galloped through life apparently without fear. Together as a family, we endured many long hours on rough Caribbean seas—the endless slam of hull to wave, the crusted rime of salt on skin—but our family stories were never as extreme as Dad's early adventures: fulfilling a bet by doing a handstand at the top of a two-hundred-foot oil derrick (and losing his job for it); numerous encounters with sharks; severing a fingertip in an Amazon piranha encounter (the fingertip stuck back on by my mother); first ascents of Huagaruncho, Nuptse, Roraima, Torres del Paine; the driving of twelve-foot boats from the island of Trinidad to its sister isle, Tobago, through the Bocas del Dragon (the Dragon's Mouth), a legendary strait separating the Gulf of Paria from the Caribbean Sea—its sea state so formidable he required a tether line to haul himself back aboard whenever he was tossed out.

Years later, my teenaged brother and sister drove a boat over this same twenty-or-so-mile route when Dad asked them to deliver a much-needed water tank. I was still a child, but I understood that this was a rite of passage of sorts. I whined about not being able to go, but my plea went unheard. Being "too young" was a constant parental refrain, one I railed against, creating fantasy adventures of my own, instead. That day the conditions were challenging and my father monitored my siblings' journey with gleeful interest. The story quickly became an inextricable part of the family repertoire.

Past narratives obviously influence future ones. In some ways I'd been raised to risk tackling the sea conditions I was looking at. But recent years of kayak guiding had reshaped my mind with an emphasis on caution and safety. And my studies had taught me about inquests: the way an accident is unravelled and decoded; the way my decisions—my credentials—would be later examined in the case of an unfortunate event. I sat in the boat, looking at the sea, my early life doing battle with my later life.

༄

It's terrible to be wrong. It is infinitely worse to sense that you are going to be wrong and to choose it anyway. We really are so close. I let myself be persuaded by Rob's argument and steer into the raging white water, the weight of my choice dragging behind me like a sea anchor. A host of invisibles rises up in my mind, doubt after doubt, each one lost to the roar of the ocean.

The rate of progress is painful. The motor groans as it pushes us up each wave and I try to avoid surfing as we fly down the other side. The route becomes serpentine as I weave between the reefs, timing my passage with the movement of swell. Some waves are manageable; others are intimidating and my eyes seek danger in every direction. Kayakers call these reefs boomers, for the sudden noise of their explosions. But crashing waves are only the second part of a boomer's equation. In the first part, the wave feeds its size by sucking the water backwards, revealing hidden rock beneath. Unsuspecting boaters can be stranded high and dry on such rocks, unable to move out of the path of the fully grown wave. This is where experience comes in. Knowledge of an area is vital. I do know this area, but as we head further out, the size and ferocity of the waves increase and the boat is pushed from all directions.

I see a swell mounting ahead. It builds and builds. When it doesn't crest, I realize that it is going to keep growing until it is monstrous. But while I'm eyeing this giant, a different wave thunders sideways at us, taking me by surprise. I accelerate through its wash just when the giant finally erupts, roaring, hurling foam and obliterating our path. For a moment the world goes white. It's hard to tell which way is up. As the spray dissipates, I see Rob's face. Suddenly, there's fear. He didn't think it would be like this. I wonder if he can read my own face. He won't see pride there. By saying yes, I relinquished the most important invisible, my judgment. But now, turning back is just as bad as going forward. Whether I am foolish, or afraid, or weak, or stupid, I am committed. A seabird shoots by and skims the waves. I picture myself doing the same and feel a surge of optimism. Skill and experience—I still have those.

I grit my teeth and grip the tiller. "If a wave tries to break on us, lean forward and hold on!" I yell. "I'll have to go full throttle, or

it'll flip us over." Rob nods and crawls, lizard-like, up to the bow to watch for hotspots. We inch forward. The trip is taking forever—at least three times longer than planned, because of the conditions and the added weight. Even though it is barely recognizable to me, I've paddled this section of coastline many times. I keep my bearings and begin counting down to the most challenging part of the trip, which will be when I nose the boat through several reefs and into a long surge channel little more than a boat's-width wide.

Eventually we get close. Two more mountains of white water to negotiate before the surge channel. There's a chance we'll make it. My fingers are clamped to the tiller, adrenaline flooding through me.

And that's when the motor loses power.

It's hard to describe what happens when you're confronted with the worst possible scenario. I am scared, but necessity keeps me functioning. I am amazed it is possible to think at all. The boat wallows in

the trough of two huge swells amid walls of water so high that I can't see land. I imagine a wave breaking on us, or worse, flipping the boat.

Suddenly, the motor starts up and we move forward again. My heart soars! But the moment is short-lived, and after a few seconds the roar fades to a whisper. A pattern begins to emerge. The motor putters. And then it fades. It putters and then it fades. My heartbeats mimic the rhythm, stopping for seconds at a stretch in nauseating moments of apnea. Each time, barely breathing, I wait for the motor to re-engage. Mentally, I conjure my list of reasons for a breakdown. I stop at the first one—gas. Of course. The gas tank is almost empty: tip it one way and the motor gets gas; tip it the other way and the motor sucks air. The swell is causing us to ascend and descend, tilting the boat and the gas tank. We're surrounded by reefs and we're running on fumes. In my early-morning planning, I hadn't factored in the extra weight and the unexpectedly long route, made even longer by the conditions. This is the era before cellphones and we don't even have a radio. I close my eyes, then open them and look at Rob, lying clamped to the bow. I look at the kayak, imagining different ways of towing a motorboat with it, all of them useless. I stop breathing, as if that will give the motor energy. Miraculously, it seems to. The boat keeps going, barely, but just enough for us to keep sliding forward—a bizarre, marine caravan of woe.

Despite poor odds, we near the final approach. I steer the hiccupping boat through the surge channel, unforgiving rock walls within touching distance either side, a huge wave thrusting up behind. The velocity of the wave shoots us through the passage into a calm half-moon bay fringed with sand. And as we skim onto the protected water, the very last vapours of gas evaporate. The motor dies.

After we unload and anchor the boat, Rob and I compare the shaking of our limbs. I can barely speak, surges of emotion washing through me: relief at our salvation, anger at Rob, exhaustion—mental and physical. But I can't let myself feel tired. I have a new problem to deal with. I'm at Echachis, with no radio and no gas. Rob helps me carry his kayak over to the calm side of the island, where I launch it and begin the hour-long paddle to Tofino. I don't know when I'll be able to drive my boat home, but I can't leave it at Echachis. I live on an island. I need it.

As I paddle, remnants of adrenaline shudder through my limbs. Ironically, I'm taking the route I originally intended to take. I marvel at the calmness of the ocean on this side of the island, but otherwise I just hack at the water as if going faster will make things better. Unable to think about what happened, I expend savage energy, flinging anger from me like so much spray. By the time I reach Tofino my legs can barely carry me and I flop on the beach like a stranded jellyfish, gazing at the placid sky, wondering what combination of elements kept the boat going until Rob and I reached safety.

Much later, after the sun has set on an otherwise perfect west coast day, I am able to reflect on the arc of my nearly disastrous journey. I examine the many small changes that caused the plan to shear away—degree by degree—from its intended course. When I think about the way I let myself be persuaded, questions rain down on me: Why did I say yes? Would a *real* west coaster tell Rob to screw off and get his own boat? Would Rob have even challenged a man that way, or do women jump a higher bar just to achieve equality? Was this about gender, or plain old strength of character?

Age-old questions. In the end, I settle on a mix. I did feel bullied into saying yes. But I was also raised by risk-takers. And because of my place in the family pecking order, the adventures usually belonged to others, not me. Like a crab clinging to my storyline, I still wanted to be chosen for the job. How deep they run, these yearnings formed in childhood. How long it takes to see them, do battle with them and learn how they apply to the mechanics of life.

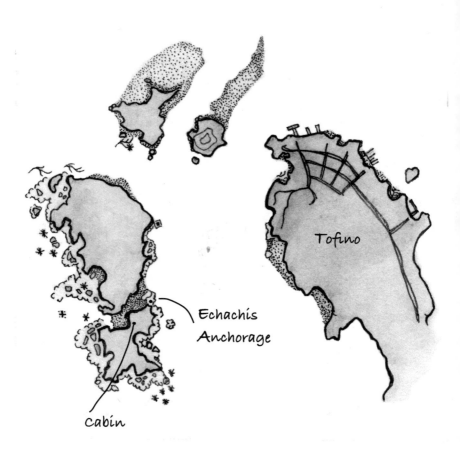

Echachis
Anchorage

Tofino

Cabin

black dark coastal night
drips with the scent of cougar
huntress. And my fear

Ghost Cat

When my flashlight died that night, I had to move gecko-style, arms and legs splayed, fingers outstretched for maximum surface coverage. At first I felt for moisture, signs of slickness and treacherous footing. But as I made my way up the rocks from the boat to the forest, my focus changed. I patted the darkness for the softness of soil and for the rough warm bark of the old Sitka spruce—my trail marker. This tree lives on a bank overhanging the shoreline. Muscular roots hold it in place, reaching through the meagre layer of topsoil to seek anchorage among boulders and crevices. The roots create a rainforest-style ladder for hands and feet. Find the tree roots and I would find the trail. From there, my journey across the island could begin.

It wasn't completely dark when I'd left Tofino by boat that night, heading for Echachis. The day had been hot and still, lacking the onshore winds that cool the coast in August. There was no fog, also unusual for August. I usually journeyed home with my partner, to our tiny shack on the far side of the island. But Carl was away fishing, so I started his small motorboat and cast off from the government dock. It was late, but the ocean had not yet released the day's light. Reflections glimmered and the silhouettes of islands were visible. I rounded Grice Point and steered into Duffin Passage. To the south, I could make out the sweeping beam of the Lennard Island lighthouse. To the southwest, I could see the dark shape of Wickaninnish Island, with Echachis close by—the dot on the semicolon. Behind the islands, black clouds rose up in the western sky, threatening a squall.

That day I'd guided four whale watching trips. I'd been on the water for over twelve hours, my ears battered by the combined noise of diesel engines and wind. On long days like that, my sanity lay in the quiet moments between trips, or those occasions when the motor was off and the deep breathing of grey whales was all I could hear. And at the end of a day, the tree-muffled silence of the forest poured an instant wash of relief and rejuvenation through me during my ten-minute walk across the island, to the west-facing beach where the cabin was situated. I craved that silence as I squinted through the darkness at the silhouetted treeline. The squall was building, but I would be home before rain fell.

As I pulled in to the bay and threw the anchor, a sudden swath of darkness rose up around me. At first I thought I had driven into the shadows cast by the tall trees. But the darkness intensified and a quick skirl of wind threw the boat sideways as I nudged the bow toward the rocks. Glancing up, I saw the cloud mass now blacking out about two-thirds of the sky. It was growing as I watched, billowing above my head. I adjusted the anchor line, grabbed my gear and climbed off the boat, slithering up the algae-clad rocks of the low-tide zone. One foot slipped and I dropped the flashlight. It stopped working, and no amount of tapping or shaking would bring the light back. I swore, jammed the light back into my pocket, then bent over to feel my way.

The first flash of lightning came as I reached the old spruce, illuminating the way. Or so I thought. I lurched into the forest, the image of the lightning-lit trail fresh in my mind's eye. Within seconds, I was on my hands and knees. The squall created such blackness I could barely trust myself to move. I began feeling for the clam-shells I'd once laid down in a moment of inspiration—fist-sized ovals of whiteness that marked the path to the cabin like Hansel and Gretel's fairytale breadcrumbs. Usually, the clamshells were visible in the gloom of twilight. Tonight they were invisible. They were recognizable by touch, however, and my fingers sought out their cool smooth shapes, so different from the other forest matter. The lightning came sooner this time, allowing me another hungry glimpse of the path. As I crawled along it, thunder cracked again, jolting me upright, hands to my ears. Crawling and scrambling, I made my way as the thunder and lightning intensified. I kept expecting rain, but it didn't come, despite the obvious humidity. The air fizzed with static, the thunder jolted and deafened, and the lightning forced me to squeeze my eyes shut, burning whitely into my retinas. I didn't worry about being struck by lightning. I assumed it would be sheet lightning, the less dangerous variety. The temperate west coast seldom becomes hot enough to produce fork lightning.

In a way, I was happy for the drama of the storm. It was a distraction. Walking through a silent forest in complete darkness can be eerie. Twice that summer, I'd been startled by animals on the trail at night. Both times the culprits had been deer, but both times their sudden bounding had sucked the air from my lungs and left me breathing hard, heart fluttering. At times like that, my mind would run with thoughts of a dear friend, Frank, whose nine-year-old son Jesse had been killed by a cougar. The cougar had simply plucked Jesse from a hollow near a trail, despite the presence of other walkers. Even though I wasn't there at the time, descriptions of that event never leave me: a boy on a trail, vanishing; a father, felled by grief, crumpling to the ground; an orange ball, lying where it fell, gleaming against wet moss.

Before I knew Frank, I had seen cougars as ghost cats, masters at the art of camouflage and secrecy. There was a sense of allure in the notion of a ghost cat; they inspired a kind of excitement. Jesse's story changed that. It showed me the reality of loss—the miles-wide chasm of shock that follows the death of a child. Frank didn't blame the cougar for its actions and he was adamant that others shouldn't, either. I didn't "blame" Jesse's cougar—a four-year-old male, shot and killed days later—but the predatory nature of cougars became harder to ignore. The ghost cat began to inhabit my mind in ways that were unhealthy. As if my mind itself were the victim, I worried about the cougar's hunting pattern: a slow, stealthy stalk culminating in a sudden attack. Tales of a cougar's silence unnerved me, too, each step soundproofed by thickly cushioned paws. And then there was the idea of the cougar's unwavering stare, the way its eyes apparently lock upon the victim in what the writer Barry Lopez once referred to among predators as "the conversation of death."

That night, I could have felt vulnerable on my hands and knees—such easy prey for a cougar. But with the storm in full flow, all creatures—cougars included—would feel vulnerable, more concerned for their own safety than in being a threat to me.

By now the cabin seemed a distant goal. I thought only of clamshells while I waited for the lightning's visual hints. My fingers became expert at reading the textural language of the path: sifting the lightness of summer forest duff; passing over the ubiquitous shoots of salal—this year's growth still soft and pliant; shrinking from the sudden cold of rocks and moss; reaching and searching for the chalky smoothness of the shells, their age marked by growth rings, ridge after subtle ridge.

The next day I was able to see where I'd gone wrong. But on this night I only knew that suddenly there were no more clamshells. At that point, I should have returned to the last shell, but I didn't. I spread my arms wide, feeling for the vegetation that bordered the trail, hoping to establish an opening. My findings were inconclusive: salal here, a tree there, nowhere an obvious path. I blundered ahead, reaching and tottering.

Perhaps it was the Norse god Thor who stopped me, his legendary battle with the serpent reaching its climax, hammers flying, the sky fractured by the sheer volume of noise. Whatever the reason,

I stood immobile with my hands clamped to my ears in a futile gesture as the blasts freighted through me. There was no pause now. The lightning came together with the thunder.

But it came in time to save me. Lost and blind, no instinct warned that I was standing at the edge of a bluff—a viewpoint overlooking the forest. Without the hissing whiteness of the flash, I would have stepped into air and fallen fifteen feet or more.

I'd often paused at this halfway point on my way home, to readjust a heavy load, or simply to appreciate the view of the forest below. Now I fought a sudden spurt of tears and threw myself back to the path I'd so quickly lost. Where once I had been calm, approaching obstacles one at a time, now I faltered. For a second I lost myself in the vastness of fear. I could have been a mother fleeing from soldiers, or a girl hiding in the dark to escape an abusive parent. I could have been anyone; it didn't seem to matter who. There in the forest, I was swept by this primal feeling, my vulnerability a sensation that linked me to human beings everywhere. I breathed deeply, not wanting to move, not wanting to remain. The force of a thunderclap flung me back to life and I started again, released.

The rest of the path home unfolded clamshell by clamshell. It seemed to take the entire night but I couldn't be sure. I only remember the end, thrashing through dense salal and falling onto the beach just as the sky lit up—with fork lightning! There it was, snaking from sky to earth, blasting what looked like an old snag on the point of the cove and lifting the hair away from my head, afro-style. Without pause, other lines of light zigzagged across the sky. I reached for the handle to the cabin and heaved the door open. Once inside, I crouched by the window, fingers grasping the sill, eyes fixed on the horizon, backpack still on.

The cabin was built near the base of a tall tree. If fork lightning were to blast the tree, the cabin would offer little protection. It was the size of a garden shed, with a clear plastic roof and a sand floor.

The walls were made of cedar planks so rough that curious Pacific wrens charmed me by hopping through the large knotholes to seek out crumbs. It was the embodiment of summer at its most simple and rewarding. My living room was the island; my bedroom was the cabin.

As I squatted by the window, I remembered my earlier, naïve presumption that the lightning would be benign. Why did I not think to check? Would I have been able to see that it was fork lightning through the dense forest? Might its hissing fingers have reached out to me as I crossed the island? Suddenly my storm journey seemed blessed, not a nightmare after all.

Javelin after javelin struck the western sea as I watched. Hours later I was still crouched, limbs stiff, body tired, but eyes and mind transfixed. Long after Thor ceased his thundering, the lightning continued. The sky was still dry. No rain had fallen. I began to think about moving, about finding the matches and lighting a candle. The irony made me wish I had someone to laugh with.

At some point I unclipped my backpack and slung it onto the floor. The hours blended into timelessness. I knew I should try to sleep so that I could be fresh for work the next day, but the idea of sleep was laughable, with the clear plastic roof inviting every blaze of light to share my space. I yawned and made myself comfortable, settling in for the long haul. I didn't expect to fall asleep, but I did—the lightning flickering over my eyes and creating a lucid dream world.

The dawn forest was soundless, foliage glistening with moisture despite the lack of rain. My surroundings were still tinged with the grey shadows of night, yet colour glowed in haphazard pockets: green here, amber there. The silence was infectious and I was pleased with my deer-like steps. For the first time in my life I walked without noise, searching the path for signs of the previous night's passage. Soon, however, the silence began to feel wrong. I longed for the usual morning chatter of birds—the breathtaking solo of the Pacific wren,

or the endless tirades of the kingfisher—anything to shatter the un-
natural quiet. Even the raucous commentary of crows would have
felt reassuring.

Where are you? I wanted to ask the birds. But I seemed unable to
speak, my vocal cords tight with a building sense of unease. I looked
around for information, as if I would find a warning scribed in tree
bark. I needed to rephrase my question to the birds, not *where are
you?* but *what are you hiding from?*

I'd once read that a cougar can see in the dark about six times better than a human. As I stood in that soundless forest, the presence of a cougar seemed certain. The idea that I was being stalked descended on me like winter frost, a rime of fear growing outward as I walked. I tried to picture where the cougar could be. I searched the path for prints and the bushes for the flick of a tawny tail. I remembered the quickness of a cougar I'd once seen, its long tail curling at the tip, like a wisp of smoke. I thought of the two cougars reported in the local newspaper earlier in the year who were swimming out from the rocks near Tofino, heading for Felice Island, or Wickaninnish. Large predators are not expected on small islands, but where there are deer and raccoons, cougars and wolves will find them. I thought of the deer roaming freely on Echachis, traversing the sandbar at low tide from Wickaninnish. They often came at sunset, cautious but undeterred by our beach fire, their dainty silhouettes decorating the evening tableau.

Other than the silence, it seemed impossible to notice clues as I floated along the trail, ears straining to pick up sounds, hands protecting my naked neck. Cougars are said to pounce from behind, sinking their powerful teeth into the victim's spine. My small hands made a poor shield, so when I found a large cedar branch, I snapped off the end and brandished it. And when I came to the viewpoint, I didn't relive the narrowly avoided fall of the past night. I only thought of the boat. And the cougar. The boat. And the cougar.

Every step took me closer to the boat. Away from the cougar.

Step. Step. Turn and look. Brandish stick above head. Be large. Seem formidable. Make noise.

Until now, I hadn't dared to make noise. The quietness held me taut, even though I knew that cougars abhor noise. I considered screaming obscenities, but if I did that, I would hear only my own voice, not the crack of a nearby twig, or the light swish of fern fronds moving. In the end, what kept me going was the light. I could see by the increasing light that I was nearing my anchorage. Any minute now I would break out of the trees, cross over the rocks, haul the boat in and climb on. And then I would be safe.

As the colours of day crept into the forest, my pace quickened and my fear lessened. I stopped holding my breath. When I saw the old spruce, I almost smiled. The horizontal branches stretched out on either side of the main trunk in a welcoming salute, defying gravity with their wide girth and obvious weight, inviting tree climbers of all ages. Seeing the Sitka spruce—my spruce—changed everything. I stopped rushing for the boat. I stopped listening for cougars. Instead, I took in the rich texture of the bark, the cushions of emerald moss and sprigs of licorice fern. I ducked under one of the branches and drew my body close to the trunk, letting its bulk shield my spine from predators. My eyes strayed to the rocks and the water, to the boat patiently waiting for me, apparently unscathed. I sighed, ushering my exhaustion and fear out into the world—shedding the heaviness of my long night, as I would have done had someone given me a hug. Somewhat restored, I turned to thank the tree and rest my hand against it. The feel of the bark under my palm is written into my memory of that moment—the moment when I turned and looked directly into the face of a cougar.

It was crouched on a branch, ready to spring, massive paws flexed.

My body coursed with cold shock. I might as well have been struck by lightning. My face was a foot from the cougar's face. I could smell the confident musk of it. As if I had whiskers of my own, I could almost pinpoint the distance between us. The short, smooth facial hairs were the colour of dried grass, while the muzzle was snowy white—a perfect foil for the electrifying kohl-rimmed eyes—eyes whose bloodlust pierced me, heart to womb.

As if waiting for me to respond—for me to participate in this conversation of death—the cougar remained motionless, its energy a tangible force. My mouth opened and the breath left my body. I screamed with all my being.

And I woke up.

The cougar's face was still a presence, still there, inches from my own. The darkness made things worse, so I staggered to my feet to find the matches. But I couldn't calm my jumping fingers, and the box fell to the floor. My attention switched to the door and I grabbed for the handle, pulling it tighter, so the dream cougar couldn't get in. Then my eyes darted to the corrugated plastic roof. It wouldn't keep a cougar out. I wrapped my arms around me and shrank into a corner of the cabin, breathing hard. Still anchored in the feel of the dream, I was sure the cougar's eyes were locked on me, its paws ready to spring. At that moment I was certain I would never again be able to walk to the boat. So how could I get help?

At no time have I been so violently overcome. Just like a cougar, my fear had stalked me, slowly and stealthily. Fear had attacked me at my most vulnerable: when I was asleep. Fear had penetrated my defenses when my guard was down. I was a victim in every sense of the word. I had no means of resistance.

❧

But the human mind is capable of great change. And as if my mind were a machine that had simply shifted gears, when true morning finally dawned, I found myself purged of fear. As I walked the path to the boat, shafts of sunlight imbued my spirits with their warmth. The forest was alive with sound and I smiled at the trill of a busybody wren. I paused at the Sitka spruce and checked the cougar branch, finding only the patina of green that comes with time. Wondering at my apparent recovery, I recalled advice from my mother—a chronic insomniac—who once counselled me to remember that what seems to happen between two and three in the morning must never be fully believed; that the time of night itself prompts the blackest of thoughts.

I did believe my dream. I still believe it now. For me, that cougar has never left the tree branch. My memory has been branded with the details of its face. I will always know how it feels to have been there, one hand on the tree, no means of escape. Just by closing my eyes, I can feel the shock.

But I did escape. And in the split-second flight to the waking world, I left my preoccupation with cougars—my fear—behind. If I really want to, I'm sure I can find it there still, somewhere near the old spruce, a heavy mass growing green with age.

Louscoone Inlet

Rose Harbour

SGang Gway

Kunghit Island

the shell's song deafens
roaring with loss. A story
of lives that should be

Scars

On my right cheek there is a fine white thread of scar tissue. Nestled among tiny veins and freckles, the scar evokes images of my father standing at the sink, face lathered in silky foam. Only three or four years old at the time, my unbroken gaze fixed on every movement of the ritual, watching foam disappear with the passing of the razor, sweep after perfect sweep. Against such whiteness, my father's face and hands shone a deep, reassuring brown. They were capable hands—hands that once saved me from a coral snake, pointed out the deep blue wings of the Mort Bleu moth, held me on the day I was born.

I remember the cold weight of the stainless steel razor and the delight of applying foam to my face. Like my father had done, I positioned the razor just so and pulled downward from my cheekbone. Predictably, blood leaped to the blade at first contact, trickling over the surface of the foam. I dropped the razor in the sink, jumped down from the stool and ran to the kitchen for help.

Doubtless I was scolded, but I don't remember it. I remember only colours: white, brown, red. I remember fascination: the slicing away of the white foam. I remember surprise: what had I done wrong?

Stories spring brightly from scars just as blood sprang from the wound on my cheek. Mostly, I think of scars as individual wounds, not wounds of the collective. But on the islands of Haida Gwaii, I found scars that conjured images so vivid I felt as if the stories were my own. I learned that not all scars are private; that some scars belong to us all.

∽

When I boarded the floatplane to the southern tip of Gwaii Haanas National Park Reserve, I thought I was prepared. Along with my sketchbooks, my bird book and my secret stash of chocolate, was a book of maps and names. The maps showed the individual houses of each old village site and the names of the families who had once lived in them. I hoped to bring history alive as I discovered this fabled coastline with every stroke of my paddle. I couldn't have predicted what a terrible thing that could be.

The islands lie 160 kilometres off the coast of northwestern British Columbia and are known for their misty beauty, Indigenous history and pockets of *refugia*—little miracles of land and life untouched by the last glaciation. The southern portion is mostly uninhabited, accessible only by boat or floatplane. Even then, travel is dependent on good weather and gentle seas, neither of which is likely. The isolation was attractive to me. I was there to help Gord, a kayak guide friend, with a week-long trip to SGang Gwaay Llnagaay, best known for the nineteenth-century village of Nan Sdins. The island is a UNESCO World Heritage Site in the southwestern part of the archipelago.

Picture yourself on a small rock, flayed by monstrous seas. Life on Nan Sdins must have been like that at times. The village is a few miles west of the main body of the archipelago, perched on an island at the very edge of the continental shelf. Here, the ocean depth slides from sixty metres to three thousand. The swell height fluctuates without warning and the average water temperature can render a person unconscious within an hour. But an abundance of seafood allowed people to thrive here and create a rich, artistic culture. My guidebook showed the locations of the renowned mortuary totem poles and longhouse remains and the names of the families who lived and died here. There was no certainty that we'd reach our destination, given the volatility for which that coastline is known, but I looked forward to seeing the historical artifacts.

The Haida Gwaii archipelago felt more remote and spacious than other places I had paddled. The inlets, with their flapping sandhill cranes, seemed to echo and vanish into the soft distance. No motorboats hurried from point to point; no other groups of kayakers dotted the horizon. In the open, moss-muffled forest along our way to Nan Sdins, occasional green rectangular outlines showed where longhouses had once stood. There is little undergrowth on the islands, due to the voracious appetites of an over-abundant deer population and an absence of wolves or cougars. In a way, it was liberating to walk among the trees of the forest without elbowing through thickets of salal or beating aside thorny salmonberry fronds. And it was curious to see history written like a language in shapes upon the forest floor.

Sitting beside one of the mossed-over rectangles, I looked up family names: *Raven Moiety, Eagle Moiety, Striped Town People, Sand Town People...* I tried to picture the beach alive with children playing. But there *were* no people in this part of Haida Gwaii. This extensive land mass was deserted. Smallpox came and life ended. The realization hit me with force. Like scar tissue, moss sealed up the wounds of history—an entire population suddenly dead. It was that simple, that brutal. The 1862 smallpox epidemic began in what was then Fort Victoria and rapidly spread up the coast, littering the Inside Passage with bodies. Seagoing Northwest Coast canoes were seen fleeing homeward, hoping—too late—to escape the disease, their occupants already stricken and putrefying. In some places the mortality rate was as high as 90 percent. In SGang Gwaay Llnagaay, the few who survived were moved to villages in the north of the archipelago. And now there was no one. The land was not spacious; it was empty. The people had been poured away and the lonely echo was that of their lost voices.

As I sat and thought about the decimation of families, the swiftness of the illness, the brutal pustules and weeping skin, a larger impression grew around me. Smallpox was over, but the wounds of contact still wept—visible, if you chose to see them. The epidemic might have changed, but people were still dying. Fresh in my mind was a young man's death several years before.

∽

I was nineteen and had lived in Canada for barely two years. My partner's family mostly lived in the village of Opitsaht, just across the water from Tofino. It was evening when a man came running into the family home. A birthday party was in full swing and we'd just cut the cake.

"Come quick," he said. "My son has hung himself."

The words jolted across the room. Then he disappeared out of the door, leaving it open.

My son has hung himself.

I could almost see those words, but it still took a few seconds to grasp what they might mean. Time slowed as I imagined a tree branch, a body swinging, hands grasping at a rope in a last-minute change of mind. There's still time to save him, I thought. And then it dawned on me: I might be the only person who could perform artificial respiration. If so, I needed to act quickly. I breathed hard and stood up. Then my legs gave out and I sat down again. I was once told that the average layperson trained in cardiopulmonary resuscitation might feel unable to take action. Suddenly, I could see why. The fear was paralyzing. What if I made a mistake? But what if someone died when I could have helped them? I stood up, shaking. I put one foot in front of the other. At the door, a tall man barred my way.

"Ladies should stay here," he said, jerking his chin toward the now-silent living room. I looked over my shoulder and saw only women and children. All the men had vanished, except this one.

"I can help him," I said. "I know CPR." He looked in my eyes, then lifted his arm.

Outside in the mid-winter darkness, I stumbled over the grass to the next house, muttering my ABCs. Airway, Breathing, Circulation, Airway, Breathing, Circulation. I wasn't sure what I was getting into, but I suspected that I wouldn't be going as far as the fourth essential: D for Deadly Bleeding. I flipped through the order of actions, the ratios of breaths to compressions. I pressed my index and middle fingers together in preparation for feeling a pulse. Please let him have a pulse! My breath rose in small, fearful clouds as I jogged. Eventually, I pushed my way through a small group of men, up the wooden stairs and into a hallway.

"Where?" I asked, with what I hoped was confidence.

A teenage boy pointed down the hall where a door stood ajar, light spilling out of it. I paused outside the door and breathed again. My hand was visibly shaking and I was still breathing hard. I tried to erase the image of the tree and prepare for a new image. Then I squeezed my eyes tight and emptied my mind of everything except CPR.

"I can do first aid," I said, entering the room, relieved to see my partner and his brother standing there. I glanced around at the ceiling, looking for a rope, or any other signs of hanging. My partner caught my eye and shook his head. "I don't think anyone can help him now, Joanna." He gestured downward to the man lying curled on the brown bedroom carpet, close to the built-in closet he had been pulled out of. The cord had bitten deeply into his neck, making a groove I could fit my little finger into. I knelt to find a carotid pulse, but cold resistance travelled from my fingertips to my brain, to my stomach. Would I feel a pulse through this? I looked at his mouth and wondered if his last words were still caught there, and if so what they were. What if my breath blew the words away? Would they flutter upward, released? Would we see them, or hear them? But this once-vital person was lying outside the realm of words. In the final reckoning, action was the only language that could express his despair.

"He's been dead for five hours," my brother-in-law said. "You won't find anything."

I made a mental readjustment as I looked up at the brothers, standing there above me, arms hanging down, faces grim. Not five minutes, as I'd previously thought. Five hours! I thought of how much brain damage can occur in such a time frame; the inevitability of death. I felt for a pulse anyway, counting the seconds but knowing that I was much too late to be of help. After a few minutes I pulled my fingers away and tucked them under my shins. I noted the small depressions my fingers had left behind and hoped my marks would fade. I looked once again at this face with its message of anguish. I'd only known my partner for a summer, yet this was the third suicide in his community, the third young man to hang himself. I'd read newspaper articles about the suicide rates in Indigenous communities across North America. I looked at the small closet they had taken him from. There wasn't room to stand up in it. He must have been kneeling.

∽

A life ending in the ultimate act of despair, and a forest, green and thriving, seemingly at peace. It was jarring to connect these two moments. Generations had passed, yet the memory of a culture still lived within the forest. I pictured hands at work—the picking of berries, stripping of cedar bark, drying of fish. I contrasted the horror of smallpox: families stricken and dying, the fear, the grief, the living tending the dying before they in turn succumbed. Until this moment, the fact of smallpox had been assigned to the rational portion of my brain. But now it migrated, reseating itself among felt experiences, joining with memories of a distraught father dashing into a house, crying for help; the memory of a young man's life, lost on a winter's night.

I looked through the forest to the shoreline, where the guests were relaxing, chatting, waiting for supper. I took a deep breath and bid adieu to the green scars. But as I walked back to camp, I knew I hadn't left them behind. They joined with me, taking up residence like an extra rib.

As the journey continued, we moved toward the outer edge of Gwaii Haanas, leaving the long, calm inlets for the exposed coastal shores. Every day's journey was evaluated and re-evaluated moment by moment as the sea state changed. Everywhere there was wildlife—tiny

tame deer, equally small bears, vibrant shoals of silver fish swirling beneath us like disco balls, while seabirds, eagles, seals and dogfish devoured them, mouthful by mouthful. We planned to cross from Louscoone Point to SGang Gwaay Llnagaay. We would visit Nan Sdins, then continue on to Kunghit Island. At every stopping point there seemed to be some sort of hint at the life before contact. I didn't mention my thoughts to the guests, but I wondered how it would feel to walk through the village site at Nan Sdins. Already, I'd seen photographs of it and knew how beautiful it was. And the greater the beauty, it seemed to me, the greater the loss.

We finally reached the island after an exhilarating passage through swells that had risen by the hour that afternoon. As we crossed from Louscoone Point, the water rose up against the stern quarter of the kayaks, shooting them forward in wild surges of acceleration. Some of the guests floundered, needing reassurance. We landed in a quiet, west-facing bay, where a dark, densely treed path led to the village. Even as we approached, goosebumps rose on my arms. And as we came into the bright clearing, the sight of the tip-tilted grey totem poles brought me to tears. I lingered at the back of the group, steeling myself for what was to come.

The village holds the ruins of ten houses and thirty-two memorial or mortuary poles. It is protected by a modern-day Haida watchman, who lives on the island during the summer. Traditionally, watchmen were seen in threes on the top of totem poles, wearing tall hats. They watched for the approach of news, good or bad. Wanagan was our watchman that day. He took his role seriously, greeting us, assessing our intentions and showing us how to behave on the island. After that, we were left to roam at will.

The guests separated, wandering alone through the remains. Each carving was unique, magnificent, achingly beautiful. Some poles had fallen, lying on the ground like tombstones in a forgotten cemetery. But cemeteries are intended for the dead; villages are built for the living. The poles were not meant to be epitaphs, but living accounts of events. The carving was perfect and precise, despite a lack of sophisticated tools. I read the stories of each house and each family. I half-managed to picture the village alive and thriving. I tried not to dwell on the brutality of disease, despite the air of sudden abandonment and all it implied. It was the decay that was so poignant. According to custom, these chapters of history close with the rotting of the poles. The poles weren't going to be replaced by fresh poles and fresh stories. They were dying, just as the people died. Just as the people continue to die. And once those old poles are gone, what then? What will that signify?

In terrible irony, through the vanishing remains of Haida villages, history became inescapably alive for me. It leaped from the past into the present, the collective scars of a people etching out the wound, as palpable as the mark on my cheek. These signs of truth, how long will the pain of them endure?

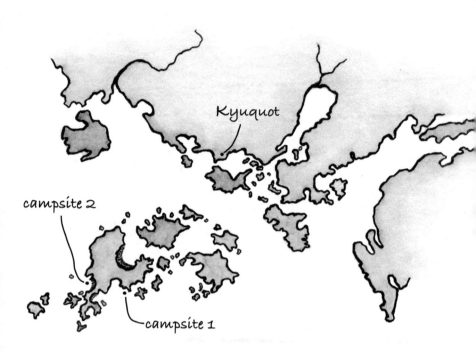

Pacific vastness
the ocean whispers, reading
her shorelines like Braille

Radio Wave

As a sea kayak guide in the nineties, I used the marine weather forecast to unravel daily intricacies of wind and waves, and plot the way these variables could be woven into my plans. There were key indicators like wind speed that were easy to anticipate. And there were more subtle elements, like fog, which operate under the most whimsical of rubrics and were never predictable. Mostly, however, careful listening to the forecast, combined with knowledge of the day's tides, could result in a workable plan. But the listening took long minutes with an ear to the VHF radio, alert for the precious words: *Vancouver Island south*. It is a testament to Murphy's Law that distraction of some sort always interrupted the vigil at exactly the moment the forecast was being delivered. The information would then be swallowed back into an endless cycle of local announcements and lighthouse weather reports. It could take half an hour to receive sixty seconds of information. Missing the forecast was a common complaint among water people, always cause for a long, drawn-out sigh.

Important as it was, however, the forecast was a tool I often saved for guiding days, preferring not to rely too heavily on technology and instead to build my knowledge of local clouds and winds. Being self-reliant is an important feature of coastal living. But some aspects of nature cannot be predicted by squinting at the sky, or the changing colour of the sea. It wasn't until October 5, 1994, while on a kayaking expedition with a friend and fellow kayak guide, that I learned how the forecast could save my life.

The trip was in Kyuquot Sound, about one hundred miles up the coast from Tofino. After camping at the terminus of a Vancouver Island logging road, my friend Cindi and I began at the Artlish River inlet and covered a distance of about twenty miles to Spring Island on the exposed west coast. Our plan was to explore the island for a day or two before continuing up the coast to Checleset Bay. It was late in the year, but deceptively summer-like. Other than the shortening October days and mornings heavy with the velvet fall of dew, the weather was warm and clear. At the very end of the long first day, we hauled the heavy boats up a steep shell beach just before darkness fell. We were on the outer coast of the island, protected from the full force of the ocean by a stockade of reefs and rocks. As an overnight stopping point it would suffice, but the next day we planned to move on.

After such a long first day, however, the next morning we were decidedly unambitious. The tent opened like a portal and we emerged into the land of Outer Shore, a land of endless motion, where—despite the windless satin sea-surface—rows of swell moved ceaselessly toward the island; where—despite the momentum of these swells, accrued over thousands of miles—the rocky barriers around us stood firm in their protective stance; where—as if not caring what lay ahead of them—the swells never once slowed in their approach. They collided with the rocks, transformed into a fine veil of breathable mist, glowed in the fragile morning light and eventually combined with the air in our lungs.

On that morning, there was silence, deep and seductive. Silence that included the many sounds of the ocean. Silence that spread into us and through us and restored us in ways that sleep could not. We moved from pause to pause, eyes locking onto the perfection of a shell, or the passage of a seabird. Our summer of work fell away, becoming a distant past, barely memorable from this new vantage point.

So it was with some reluctance that we began to prepare for the day ahead. The small, steep beach, at least twenty feet deep in mussel shells, was topped with a sharp ledge and made an awkward landing, especially with the heaviness of our boats provisioned with two weeks of supplies. If we were to stay and enjoy Spring Island to the full, we would have to move. Half a mile to the west lay a low neck of land dividing two calm bays, each one blessed with a protective corral of rocks. Depending on the wind direction, we could launch or land from either side of the tombolo, and take shelter from opposing winds. The pond-calm bays quickly opened out onto the deep ocean, but once our laden boats were launched this wouldn't be an issue. Most importantly, the chart showed a trail that would allow us to explore the island on foot and stretch our ever-cramped kayaking legs. As the drops of dew evaporated from our tent fly, we lounged in the sun, savouring the moment of languor and discussing the day ahead. Eventually we began to make breakfast.

My travelling companion, Cindi, was a long-time friend and fellow guide with a penchant for baking. Together, she and I had explored many wild places, either by kayak or on foot. Our love for these adventures was a hub of connection, remote trips being the high points, charted like constellations, star to star. We travelled together with ease, neither of us too attached to our goals. Where I might have eaten cereal for breakfast, Cindi often preferred something she could create. On this morning, we divided the chores without much discussion. I made a small fire while she cracked eggs and stirred batter for pancakes. The fire slowly burned down to the coals needed for pancakes, and as we began eating them we turned on the handheld VHF radio to hear the forecast. The softness of the morning and the fact that we were only going to travel half a mile made the listening seem a waste of valuable batteries. But for some reason—if only our extreme isolation—we chose to listen anyway.

There are times in life when situations do not fit with one another; their overlay is awkward, no sharing of common ground. On that beach, on that morning, the words "pan-pan" emanating from the VHF were surely a mistake. Repeated three times, pan-pan is marine terminology for a state of urgency, a not-to-be-missed message. It often precedes the announcement of a hazard, a boat in distress or a mariner in jeopardy. From our place on the beach, it seemed impossible that any of those things could occur. It was with complete inability to digest the information that we took note of a tsunami warning, following a magnitude 7.7 earthquake in northern Hokkaido, Japan—the tsunami expected to reach BC's coast at 15:30 hours.

In the surreal moment of the announcement, I pictured the endless rows of swell travelling across the Pacific from Japan. I imagined those swells increasing to many-storeyed heights and valley-deep troughs. I imagined them rolling right over Spring Island, this completely flat island that lacked even a single contour line. Small, cold stones slid down my throat to settle on top of the pancakes in my stomach. It was eleven o'clock. It could take us an hour to pack up. We would then have three hours left to paddle to safety *if* the tsunami arrived on time.

What if it arrived early? There didn't seem to be an answer to that.

We decided to head to the village of Kyuquot, about five miles to the northeast. Surely Kyuquot would have a preplanned safe place for escaping tsunamis? The village was situated at the bottom of a steep hillside. At the very least we might find people there. That in itself would be comforting.

We packed up the boats in record time (much less than an hour) and launched from the steep shell beach. For a moment my boat balanced on the ledge, its heavily weighted bow jutting horizontally into air, stranded by the wave I'd hoped would float me. Helpless, I waited for the next wave and cringed as an audible crack came from the frame. This was no time for boat repairs. But the wave carried me away from the beach, my thrashing paddle strokes fuelled by the bizarre mix of pancakes and panic. It took a few hundred yards to relax and begin pacing myself for the journey ahead. We left the protective stockade of rocks and reefs, going back the way we had come the night before. I checked my cockpit for signs of water entering from a crack in the kayak's frame. There was nothing. Yet.

As we paddled, Cindi and I pooled our knowledge of tsunamis. I'd learned about tsunamis in geology and to me they existed in the realm of theoretical events. Even though I knew a subduction zone ran along coastal British Columbia, I had no sense of tsunamis as a threat to my personal safety. My casual attitude had been bolstered by Frank Harper's story "The Great Bogus Two-Inch Tsunami," published in *The Sound* newspaper. The story was a series of interviews with Tofino residents, detailing the hilarity and lack of seriousness with which they greeted a tsunami that never arrived.

There are times when the world changes, little by little. And there are times when it changes suddenly, radically, unalterably. That's how it's been for me with tsunamis. When—much later in life—the devastating earthquake and tsunami laid waste to northern Japan in 2011, Earth's catastrophic possibilities became inescapably real for me. That tsunami and the Boxing Day tsunami in the Indian Ocean were shocking for their combined death toll. But they also carried with them vivid, live-camera footage of the events—images which spread around the world at lightning speed, bringing horror and sadness to people everywhere. The news became a kind of Pandora's box to me. I tried not to look at the footage, but eventually I couldn't help myself. Afterward, I felt as if the images themselves had crawled into my brain, making their home in previously inactive regions. Perhaps it was worse because I live on a floathouse. It seemed so real, so possible. By then I also had a daughter, which increased the emotional understanding of loss. The notion of tsunamis became impossible to ignore. First, the tsunami sirens arrived, making it tricky to walk my local beach without being reminded that an earthquake might strike. Then, simple acts like beachcombing became tinged with poignancy:

if these found objects could speak, what tales of grief and loss would they tell? What of the child to whom this toy belonged?

Still sculpted into my brain is the photograph taken by Pete Clarkson, a Parks Canada warden and marine debris artist, who visited Japan after the 2011 tsunami. The photo is of a mangled metal staircase, reaching out to the sky, connected to nothing. It was erected days before the tsunami, to evacuate school students to higher ground. Nothing remains of the school, so completely was it washed away. But on that fatal day, every child's life was saved by that stairway. Would there be stairways such as this one for my own child? I wondered.

These experiences have changed my outlook so profoundly it has become impossible to imagine the state of innocence that preceded them. The carefree age of Not Thinking About Tsunamis is over for me. I cannot recreate it. But as I relive the paddle from Spring Island to Kyuquot, I can remember how I felt then, still untainted by familiarity with tsunamis, the wash of reactions: incomprehension, practical planning, the mental turmoil of imagined thoughts, the fear. In the pre-Internet age, those few words over the radio waves were all the knowledge we had.

The tsunami was due to arrive at 3:30 pm. If we paddled fast, we hoped to reach Kyuquot by 1:30. But the conditions were challenging. Was it the earthquake in Japan that made the sea-state so volatile and caused the swell to rise to such dramatic heights? Already pumped with adrenaline, we paddled hard and negotiated the swell as it peaked and crested over invisible rocks and rebounded from the land with a sloshing effect. We dodged white water and slid through gaps in surf breaks. Not until we reached the lee of Spring Island did the conditions ease. We continued heading northeast, propelled by the image of the tsunami's passage across the ocean. Where was it now?

As we passed Aktis Island a man on shore began waving his arms in the traditional signal of distress. We wondered if he just

wanted to tell us about the tsunami, or if he actually needed help, but a distress signal is a distress signal, so we took a detour and paddled over to see him. "There's a tsunami should be here in a couple hours," he informed us when we finally reached him. "You shouldn't be on the water." We agreed. When we told him our plan, he nodded. "Probably won't amount to much anyways. Last one just made the tide run harder. Was like a river back here." He gestured to the narrow passage we had just come through. "A few boats got sunk. That was about all." The man's speech was soft and drawling, lacking all urgency. He was poised to share a world of personal experiences and we could have stayed for hours, chatting about tsunamis past. But our preoccupation was with tsunamis future. We thanked the man and paddled away, wondering how much time the detour had added to our journey. Wondering if tsunamis arrive early.

A few minutes later a helicopter buzzed overhead, then circled back and crouched above us, casting its net of windborne chaos. The roar of wind and rotors combined to override a buzzing crackle of information being broadcast by some kind of loudspeaker. If the crew were telling us about the impending tsunami, their efforts were unintelligible. Sign language was impossible because our hands were glued to the paddles, busily negotiating the wind hazard created by the rotors. Eventually the helicopter moved on, its message lost in the vortex of wind and spray.

The good intentions of local people were expressed several more times as our journey was delayed by further helpful warnings from boaters. Increasingly, we kept our communications brief, pointing to Kyuquot and miming a rapid paddle stroke. We spoke less to one another, the rhythm of our arms building as the minutes passed. It was with great relief that we entered Kyuquot Harbour with forty-five minutes to spare.

Kyuquot is a community of First Nations people whose lives revolve so completely around the water that almost anyone would be likely to know where we should go, and—we hoped—what we should do with our kayaks. We had not anticipated the total absence of human life that greeted us. No children playing at the water's edge, no adults packing up the last precious items of a home, not even a tail-wagging dog, oblivious to its uncertain future. We whooped and hallooed, spirits sinking as our voices echoed through the desert of empty houses. Even the general store on Walter's Island was closed. Everyone had been evacuated. But to where? Bewildered, we stood on the government dock and used the payphone to call home. Taking the time to update our whereabouts seemed both frivolous and urgent, but it was while we were doing this that two people emerged from a large white seine boat, moored at the dock. Divining our situation, they invited us to ride out the tsunami with them at sea—kayaks and all. In the way of true seafaring people, they didn't doubt the wisdom of this choice, and their authority brought the direction we needed. In tsunamis, large boats fare better in deep water, where the rebound effects and the steepness of waves are much diminished. This husband and wife duo was prepared for the tsunami in every way conceivable, from the on-board satellite TV to the full fuel and water tanks and the freshly baked muffins.

Just as we had earlier emerged through our tent door into the outer shore environment, here again we ducked under the doorsill, and stepped down the ladder into a cozy, burrow-like space where fear for future moments was left behind. We were seated on a plush couch and plied with tea and coffee. We learned about each other's lives as we watched the latest tsunami updates on colour TV. The projected size of the wave seemed to shrink with every update. By the time 3:30 rolled around, we were leaning over the dock, examining the water for any hint of a wave. That was when the newscaster announced that the tsunami warning had been cancelled.

Much later, I learned that eleven people had died in that earthquake, some buried beneath a military hospital, others felled by debris as they attempted to flee their homes. The earthquake had been sudden, with no quiet rumblings to foreshadow it. Lives had changed rapidly that day and it was interesting to think that our own experience mirrored some small part of that—the change in plans, the adrenaline, the racing minds, the exhaustion. More lasting was a perception of the ocean's ability to reflect and speak the language of Earth, that day's suddenly turbulent sea-state a direct communication, if only I had been literate enough to read it.

The approach of evening ushered us back to Spring Island. Our fisher friends had urged us to stay at the dock, but we'd already been away too long, and valuable wilderness moments were being lost. The respite had given me time to examine the hull of my boat, where I found a visible crack. Surprisingly, to this day it has never leaked.

Two hours of paddling later, we arrived at the beach we had been aiming for that morning. We'd travelled more than ten miles to get there, encountering taxing conditions and a realm of unforgettable experiences along the way. We set up camp in the quickening October dusk, longing for food and sleep. And as a way to round off the day, we turned on the handheld VHF radio, some small part of us still doubting our safety. At the words *pan-pan*, the cold stones resurfaced in my gut. Not again! I couldn't believe what I was hearing. We had finally set up camp. The boats were unpacked. Heading back to Kyuquot in the conditions we'd just negotiated seemed not only overwhelming, but also foolhardy considering the darkness and our fatigue. Cindi and I stared at each other in the lantern light, listening with dreadful anticipation. And then we heard the final words "is expected to reach our coast at 15:30 hours."

I don't know why Coast Guard Radio failed to report the cancellation of the tsunami that night. I wish they could have known the panic it threw us into. But while I begrudged them the error, I looked at our small handheld radio with newfound respect. Its airborne voice had transformed this remarkable day. The starry night sky competed for my attention, beckoning me to think only of the universe and its beauty, but the radio's reminder drew me across the remarkable whispering ocean to the coast of Japan and the people whose lives—like mine—were held in balance by only the merest threads.

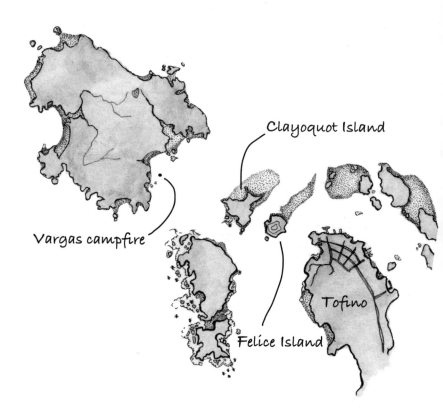

Clayoquot Island

Vargas campfire

Felice Island

Tofino

*September beachfire
reaches through darkness, calling
to faraway stars*

One Bright Star

There is an allure to darkness—an exhilaration that accompanies the sudden arrival of the unknown, the sense of extraordinary potential. Perhaps that's what prompted me to paddle away from the beach on Vargas Island one late-summer night. Or perhaps I was prompted by nostalgia for my equatorial childhood, where evenings were warm and life continued after darkness fell. In Trinidad, I loved the night wind at Mayaro Beach, the pale onslaught of breakers and the back-and-forth mutter of coconut branches. In darkness, the wind seemed different on my face. I smelled its dense salinity. I relished its fresh warmth. In a recurring dream—one I can still conjure—my young self goes night-walking beyond the safety of the yard, down a sea-ward path where I linger at the edge of the beach, my fingers seeking out the ringed bark of a coconut tree. A temptress appears, twice my height, her cool hand tugging mine. I resist, clutching the tree and looking to the unlit porch of the house for help, where—deep in conversation—my parents talk about grown-up things, watching me but never coming to my aid. The dream always ends with my hands slipping over the dry bark as I begin to let go. Night—the pull of her.

And then there was the festival of Diwali, when Hindu families placed tiny clay lamps at regular intervals along walls, railings and stairways. They split lengths of bamboo, bending and twisting them into shapes along which to place the lamps—confronting the wilderness of spiritual darkness with a symbolic fantasia of inner light, each flame so small, so bright, so imbued with meaning. I remember the simple red clay cups, their string wicks anchored in pools of oil. I remember the thrill of our nighttime excursions to see the displays.

But night's greatest secret was more exotic even than Diwali. With no calendar date to pre-empt it, we watched and waited for the nocturnal blossoming of the Queen of the Night, the scented white cactus whose straggly limbs were woven into the hibiscus hedge at the bottom of the garden. Daily, the flower buds would tempt us with their growth, but only my father seemed certain of their opening night. We tiptoed down the hill behind the flashlight's yellow path. And there we stood, waiting like penitents for the miraculous light of the unfolding flower, the night air feeding our excitement and amplifying our held breath. Our cheeks glowed in the bright face of the queen, our gasps caught in the explosion of scent as the petals spread open like fingers, offering up the pollen-tipped stamens—the naked heart of the plant. That this magnificent creation only lasted until morning exemplified the strangeness of time and the fleeting nature of life. I remember wondering if plants grieve.

Perhaps these special childhood moments increased my attraction to darkness, or perhaps the attraction is universal, felt by many. Regardless, paddling six kilometres at two in the morning didn't seem like an unusual choice. My campfire friends encouraged me to stay, for reasons of companionship more than safety. But the idea of waking up in my own bed had taken hold.

The moon was sinking toward the Vargas treeline as I hauled the warhorse of the kayak rental fleet down to the water's edge. *Bucephalus* was an ancient double kayak my place of work had loaned me for its front cockpit, which perfectly fitted my dog, Sweetheart. She stepped aboard with her customary elegance and waited while my mind played over the plusses and minuses of leaving. That night's fire had reached a point of perfection, blushing with the shifting hues of radiant coals. Shadow puppets danced against the glow as fireside fellows settled and resettled themselves, their murmured late-night thoughts punctuating moments of quiet and contentment. It was a peaceful scene, one I wanted to be part of. Yet somehow the contentment of the following morning was more important to me. I didn't want the chaos of a hurried departure. I didn't want the noise and bustle of a busy Tofino, inevitable when I returned *Bucephalus* to the kayak store. I wanted to wake in my own bed, far from the sudden roarings of floatplanes and charter boats, cars and people. On mornings when I woke up at home I slipped naturally into the mode of the slough, gliding through the off-grid day with ease. But if I arrived home at midday, the transition was less fluid. There was the inevitable unpacking, followed by a protracted sense of dislocation before I finally settled in. On partial home days, the wilderness drug was less potent. And that realization is what propelled me to grasp the toggle and move the kayak into the water.

I left quietly, not wanting to draw attention to my desertion. North of me, the lights of Kakawis twinkled on the flat water; to the southeast, I could see the blinking green light of a buoy. I took the most efficient route, crossing Father Charles Channel to the westernmost point of Clayoquot Island and adjusting my angle of glide to accommodate the sideward push of the tide. At Clayoquot I would take the proverbial fork in the road and choose either an outer or inner route—the outer route exposed to the ocean, but possibly quicker; the inner route glass calm, but with an area of mudflat which might not be deep enough for me to cross. I gave myself up to the sweetness of the moment and thought it likely that I would choose the outer route. Sweetheart sighed and settled herself, sinking into the seat and resting her chin on the rim of the cockpit, her ears forming two pale triangles. Behind me, the quarter moon became yellow as it neared the horizon. There was barely a hush from the shore waves as I paddled away.

With the departure of the moon, my surroundings grew darker, lit only by the stars. The air was sharp and my hips rolled side to side as the swells palmed the kayak's hull, lifting it up and sliding it down, as if passing me hand to hand. I considered the alchemy of the Milky Way, the bright spiral of gasses and dust smeared across the sky above me. Just a few weeks earlier I'd watched the Perseid meteor shower from a canoe, lying on my back and drifting up the slough on the flooding tide. Back then the stars were rocketing to and fro like popcorn, but now they showed more restraint, pulsing with clear light from their fixed locations. Ahead, one bright star beckoned me onward.

Partway across the channel the green light of the eastern buoy seemed to grow dim. It flashed, then vanished, flashed again, then vanished completely. Perhaps it wasn't working properly, or perhaps the disappearance was related to my moving position. Sightings on the water are difficult that way—visible from one angle, invisible from another. I kept my course and paddled onward. But when the glow of light from Tofino also disappeared, I knew something was up. If it was fog, I couldn't see it. And the foghorn hadn't yet called out its arrival. I considered taking the compass from my life jacket and placing it on the taut apron of my spray skirt. But my compass was a fiddlesome thing, hard enough to see in daylight. If I flashed my headlamp at the compass I would be night blind, unable to locate any visual bearings. Instead, I let down the rudder, determined my line of travel and locked my feet in position on the pedals.

That night the fog moved with such stealth and swiftness that the foghorn didn't boom until my world was completely obliterated. I watched each landmark vanish, one after the other. First the Tofino peninsula, then Wickaninnish Island, and lastly—bit by bit—my landmark, Clayoquot Island. With nothing ahead of me, I looked up, finding that one bright star still visible above me. It was flanked by two smaller stars, not part of any constellation—simply the only stars left in my visual range. Together they made a triangle with the brightest at the apex. The sight of them bolstered my courage, reassuring me that the fog was still only a very thin layer.

Fast-moving fog is often accompanied by wind, but the fog on this night had no running mate. The surface of the water was unruffled and the swells pushed me onward as if nothing had changed. Their unbroken rhythm didn't allow me time to stop. I paddled forward, keeping the stars in a triangle above me, appreciating their persistence. From time to time the smaller stars in the triangle faded from view, obscured by wisps of fog, but always the bright star gleamed. It wasn't Polaris—the North Star—but its celestial guidance seemed trusty as any compass. I didn't paddle harder or faster. I didn't worry where I was going, or whether I would get lost. Ahead of me, the peaks of Sweetheart's ears vanished as she sank lower in the cockpit, only the tip of her nose visible. She wasn't worried, either.

For fifteen minutes I paddled this way, my gaze drawn to the eastern sky, my ears hearing only the one-two slice of paddle through water. When the sound of crashing waves finally became audible,

I knew I was just where I'd hoped to be. By then the two smaller stars had vanished completely and even the brightest star was sometimes fading. But now that I was nearing land I had sea sounds to guide me. The surf became louder and dark rocks rose up ahead, marking the western tip of the island. It was time to choose my route. Technically, the inner route was safer: it offered protection from surf and swell—calm passage over shallow eelgrass beds. But if the tide were too low, I would have to go around these areas, following an unknowable perimeter. The trip could be long, made much longer if I got stranded or lost.

I chose the outer route, drawn partly by the sound of the surf. In the absence of visibility, sound meant knowledge. The louder the crash, the closer the shoreline. And unless I strayed from the source, this simple form of echolocation couldn't be taken from me. I liked that. Paddling more slowly, I inched to the right, heading to the first outer beach.

It was harder than I'd thought. The beach faces southwest with a dumping shore wave. Even at a distance from the beach, propagating waves mount steeply, peaking but not always cresting. I swung out as wide as I dared, not wanting to lose the dark mass of the land, but a wave still took me by surprise, accelerating beneath me with a thrilling surge. *Bucephalus* made an excellent steed, so wide and stable that even the sideways thrust of the breaker didn't wake my sleeping canine passenger. I moved further offshore. Or where I thought offshore was. I could barely see—deprived not of sight, but of sights. I could see my hands on the paddle, I could see the forward cockpit and, with effort, the bow. Everything else, however, was a mystery, not at all resembling its daytime self.

I wasn't deprived of other senses, however; in fact, I was immersed in a sensory language, straining to identify disparities in sounds, shocked at my illiteracy. The planet has spoken for millennia, yet only now was I paying proper attention to the words. Within the general assonance of sea sounds, I listened for specifics: the relentless soldiers' march of the beach waves; the cannonade of swells breaking over rocks; the twirling waltz of water surging—but not breaking—around reefs or kelp beds. Each of these phrases was useful in its own way, telling how close I was to safety, and to danger.

At the jutting point between southwest- and southeast-facing beaches, I manoeuvred around a collection of rocks. With visibility, I would have sought out the gap between these rocks, waited out the biggest waves, and darted through the gap in a brief surge of glory. Now I virtually tiptoed, not wanting to stray from my landmarks, nor get too close. A wave arrived out of the blackness like a magic carpet, sluicing me forward. I dug the paddle aft, fighting to halt the momentum of the kayak as a shape rose before me. The bow glanced off a rock, turning the boat parallel to the next wave, but by then I was in full reverse, just able to avoid being thrown sideways on the reef.

Despite the sudden challenge of the journey, I was surprised at my lack of fear. The route was demanding but stimulating. I knew it well, having paddled it day after day, season after season. Seen through the filter of fog and darkness, it was a puzzle with most of the pieces missing. And the fragments I could see were untethered to the whole, like images cropped from a composition. Each rock or kelp bed needed me to identify it, catalogue it and place it on a mental map, along which I could plot my guessed-at position. My brain whirled and spun with effort. Anticipating the next few kayak lengths always seemed to be the hardest task. The puzzle neared completion as I reached the last obstacle, a string of rocks jutting out to the south.

Here, I dithered. I didn't want to go all the way around the point. Doing so would expose me to greater swell and a longer, more challenging route. If I could find a little gap between the rocks, one passable at the present level of the tide—if I could shoot through it and thereby cut the corner—if I could do all this, and come out in one piece, I would be so much closer to safety. There were two possible options. I just had to find them. I turned the bow southward and moved parallel to the rocks, slowing my pace and whetting my senses. I would have missed the first passage if a wave hadn't broken through it, pushing me sideways. I remembered that the wave always broke on the south side of this little gap, spilling over a reef. Only in big swell did the wave occlude the whole channel. I turned to face the rocks and tried to see the gap. Twice more, white water cascaded toward me out of nowhere, but by the third time I was prepared. As soon as the whiteness passed under my hull, I heaved on the paddles, forcing the boat into the space and—miraculously—through it.

Through! I wanted to cheer, but I still needed to hear the world around me. Turning north again, I picked my way along the edge of Van Nevel Channel, nearing the Tofino Harbour with every paddle stroke. I began to think about the next part of the journey: whether I'd be able to boat home after returning the kayak. It seemed unlikely, which was depressing. I had just decided to think about that later when I glided out of the fog.

I gasped, looking over my shoulder. Behind me, the fog bank stood like a blank wall, lacking any sense of movement. I was near the private dock at Clayoquot Island. Above, stars speckled every part of the sky, my guiding star still bright among them. Ahead, the harbour gleamed with shapes and reflections. Lone Cone Mountain rose up from the lowlands of Meares Island like a child's cut-out, slightly imperfect at the top. The lights of Opitsaht cast long, shimmering reflections, as did the lights of Tofino. It was just like Diwali, the street lights placed at regular intervals, illuminating the urban wilderness. Ahead of me, two white triangles reappeared as Sweetheart sat up and took in her surroundings.

I thought of the conditions I'd just left. There was no way to compare the two realities. I could have taken a calm route home without suffering a moment of self-doubt. But would I have had the same sort of connection with the ocean? Out there, the sea whispered with comings and goings, warnings and lullabies. Those sounds were now alive in me—a freshly minted melody.

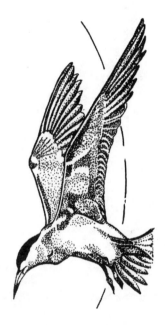

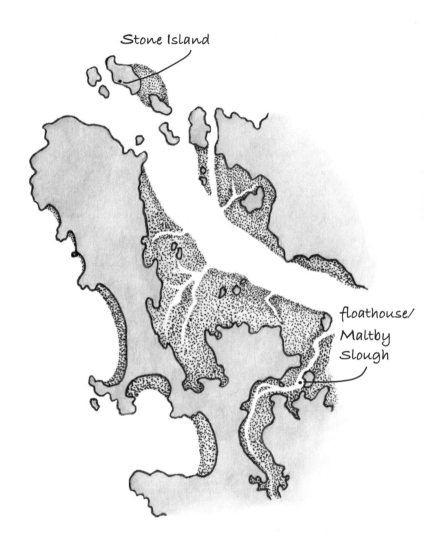

*winterstorm shrapnel
speckles the sky. My breath
roars in the silence*

Balancing Act

I'm half an hour from Tofino, in Maltby Slough, where my floathouse is now anchored. And I'm standing on the dock, staring at snowflakes falling fast, as if weighted. They are large as silver dollars, burying my small floating empire and veiling the wilderness beyond it. My open boat is moored to the floathouse and filling with snow. I search for the best tool with which to remove it, finally fixing on a dustpan. I'm used to bailing, but shovelling is another matter. With this blizzard I am completely cut off.

I wasn't born a floathouse dweller. In fact, not until I arrived in Tofino did the word floathouse enter my vocabulary. Trinidad had been too exposed to the Atlantic, without the protected waters that make calm anchorage possible. In England, the closest equivalent was a narrow boat, a beautiful gypsy boat, horse-drawn along canalways and ornamented with bright scrolls of paintwork.

My partner and I first moved onto a floathouse at the end of a cold and particularly miserable winter, after I'd been in Tofino for about two years. It had been a trying time—a grand toppling of dominoes, situation by situation, down a precarious line. It began much earlier with the unplanned arrival of a large white dog tied to a pickup truck in our parking lot, her owner swept by a situational crisis. First, Carl and I looked after her for a week, then a month. After three months of smuggling "Sweetheart" into our no-pets apartment, and beguiled by the many charms her original owner named her for, our decision making ceased including prudence and included only sentiment: we wanted to keep her, name and all.

The snow is still falling. Where before it fell straight down, now it arrives in flourishes, skirling in the gathering wind. Beyond the opaque cloud of it, alder branches crack under the sudden weight and fall into the water, splashing loudly. A sibilant swishing noise begins to grow as snowflakes build on the water, layer upon layer, swirling in the tide. I bail the boat of snow for the second time, wondering how long the storm might last. For now, the island behind the floathouse is sheltering me from the southeast wind. As the storm picks up, however, no obstacle will stop the strongest gusts from finding their way in here.

We became aware that Sweetheart had reached adolescence when Sparky—the gentle giant of Tofino's canine world—arrived on the lawn below our second-floor balcony and began a serenade that would have humbled Romeo. Besotted, he settled in for the duration of Sweetheart's fertility, greeting us whenever we left the building and escorting us wherever we wanted to go. Sparky stayed despite the many midnight pleas for quiet by sleep-deprived residents. He stayed (albeit switching to *sotto voce*), despite the sudden throwing of shoes and other objects that accompanied those cries. And he stayed until no amount of dog smuggling could conceal our misdemeanour and we were asked to leave. But it was summertime and Carl suggested moving out to Echachis Island, his family's traditional territory. The idea beckoned with a promise of outer-coast beauty. All we would need was a roof to keep the rain off. We'd build a cabin, no problem. There was now no question of parting from the dog, so instead we parted—blithely—with the only stable housing Tofino had to offer: *adios Sin City, we're moving to paradise!* Of course, anything beyond summer living at Echachis was impossible given the rudimentary set-up of our hastily built shack. And so when summer ended, we joined

the infamous Tofino Shuffle and searched for pregnant-dog-friendly housing—the sum total of which was Tom Curley's generous offer of his boat, the *Alannah C.*

The storm is progressing and my friend's words ring in my ears—casual words, words not reserved for teaching but for storytelling, words that could impart wisdom, if only I knew what to do with them. His words tell of blizzards sinking floathouses up north, camp workers using snow rakes to lighten the load on floathouse rooftops. Snow is a rarity in Clayoquot Sound. And without this storm, his story would seem irrelevant. But now, I'm looking at my roof. And one by one, the words are sinking in...

It was two in the morning at Fourth Street Dock, and the *Alannah C* was rocking violently in a southeast storm when Sweetheart leapt into the front berth and began the kind of panting that could only mean one thing. I soothed her until daylight, then moved her to the covered back deck where I'd set up a tarp-lined puppy corral, replete with privacy curtains, straw and a large, comfy bed. And so the pups arrived, one every half hour, seven silent balls of whiteness—silent, that is, until a few weeks later, when the joys of parenthood began to pale against the sounds of their nocturnal yips. So when we were offered the opportunity to house-sit for a friend—who not only had a garden, but also a safe garden shed, perfect for the ever-more-voluble and Houdini-like pups—we moved with alacrity. That the opportunity was a gift is impossible to deny. I probably owe it my sanity. But after a summer on Echachis, the winter routine of indoor life—with laundry, refrigerator, comfy beds and television—began to produce a strange effect on me. Maybe it was the reality of my new life, so far from home and family, immersed in the new-to-me culture of my partner. Maybe it was just the mundane nature of life on a street. Whatever it was, something was missing. And I didn't know what it was.

One by one the puppies left home to live with their respective families. I didn't have time to mourn them because our host returned and we had to move. We moved to a little house built snugly on a fibreglass barge at the end of a crab fisherman's dock near Strawberry Island. The floathouse belonged to Mike, a bearded ex-American with a voice like a didgeridoo and a talent for the washtub bass. Mike preferred to winter in town and allowed us to occupy his vacant space. On the first night, I was sitting outside watching the swirl of the tide when a pod of orcas came by. In the dark, I counted five of them by the sounds of their blows alone. And just like that, as if they breathed new life into me, the feeling that something was missing slipped away.

I'm standing on the dock, looking at my Christmas-cake roof and its foot-thick layer of snow. In my mind's eye, marzipan figurines—red scarves flying—sled past the chimney, over the eaves and out into the storm. The wind shrieks and pounces on the figures, gobbling them up. More snow falls and the layer of roof icing grows thicker. I stop looking at the roof and begin to look at the waterline of my house, where the sub-floor fascia board is now several inches underwater.

Summer came and we moved again, this time to the cabin on Stone Island, directly across from Tofino. And it was there, for the first time, I decided to take matters of accommodation into my own hands with the help of a financial windfall I'd received. I contracted a builder to make a floathouse. I didn't know where we were going to put it, but I knew one thing: I was tired of living in other people's homes, on other people's terms. And I wanted to live on the water. Carl and I had been beachcombing each winter and had amassed a floating herd of logs. They followed us obediently as we towed them to their fate at the Vargas Island sawmill. In exchange for half the wood, Neil Buckle milled them into beams and boards so that, piece by piece, the house became a reality.

The process was not problem-free, however, and the plan changed as I let myself be persuaded against a low-profile, single-storey structure, to a higher-profile peaked roof with an upstairs loft. But while I was envisioning a compact building with a small loft, the builder (a large man given to sturdy construction) had chosen eight-foot ceilings upstairs and down. The resulting post-and-beam house frame was beautiful. It was also too heavy for the float it was built on. Worse, on two sides it was built to the very edge of the float, making the house tippy and susceptible to wind gusts. As the float sank into the water, work slowed until no further weight could be added. When I ended the contract and towed the house home to Stone Island, it had a beautiful shake roof, a loft floor, a staircase and little else. It also had an unresolvable problem: insufficient floatation. The flat-bottomed float didn't allow barrels of air to be added to it; they would roll out. There was no local technology that would allow for the addition of foam and there was not yet an Internet with which to search out new ideas. The beams were in the water, where they would be destroyed by shipworms. And I was out of funds and out of luck. For over a year, the house wallowed at anchor, regarding me through the baleful eyes of its empty window frames. I wallowed, too, the house my dismal anchor.

The water numbs my already stiff fingers as I check each corner of the house and monitor the slow descent of the beams in the water. I fumble with the tape measure, throwing it aside and grabbing a piece of kindling instead. I don't need specifics, I need an overview: low risk, medium risk, high… The kitchen corner is lowest—one of the floatation tanks has some kind of slow leak. At this moment it is an inch lower than the rest of the house, more than a hand's width down.

It was Rod Palm—shipwreck diver and local legend—who uncovered a trove of floatation tanks that were not cylindrical, but square. What's more, they were free, save the cost of shipping and the diver to fill them with air. Rod installed them one bright fall day, my spirits rising with every inch of freeboard on the house. For the first time in months, I dared to think about building. I pictured siding and windows. I pictured our bed in the loft. Infused with hope, I could barely sleep and—childlike—I ran to the window in the morning to see how the house was doing. I gasped. The previous night everything had been perfectly level. Now, the house was listing heavily; the apex of the roof was off-centre, pointing to ten o'clock. One push and it would heel over. I sprinted down the long ramp, leaped in my boat and sped to the Norvan—the original wooden North Vancouver ferry, dry-docked on the shoreline of Strawberry Island—home to the Palm family. I idled my boat below their open kitchen window while Rod unravelled my panicked words, puffing on his pipe and squinting across the harbour at the floathouse. That morning he explained how saturated wood becomes lighter over time as it dries out. He readjusted the floatation, measuring each corner of the house. Once again, he left it perfect. Once again, by nightfall the house was listing, this time the other way. That night, I listened for every wave and breath of wind, willing the house to survive until morning. Rod fixed the floatation again and this time it stayed level. But now I saw the terrible irony: with buoyancy, the house was less stable than ever. And if just one of the floatation tanks gave out in the middle of a storm…

The storm is picking up, slamming the house with gusts. I shudder as the house heels over, holding my breath until the gust subsides and the house swings upright again. The added weight on the roof has changed the centre of gravity. The moment of return becomes longer and more painful to endure as the power of righting is diminished. The gusts push the house and the lines stretch tight in sudden jerks, as if the feet of the house are being pulled out from underneath it. I reel backwards, or sideways, flinging my arms outward. I imagine mounting the rickety ladder and climbing onto my steep roof. There is no way I can do it. The snow will have to stay there.

When swallows build a nest, if the consistency of the mud is too granular or too dry, the nest falls off the wall and crumbles on the ground. The swallows rebuild quickly, before it's too late to produce a second clutch. Seasonal urgency triggers persistence and innovation. Eventually, the swallows will get the recipe right, create a sturdy nest and produce one or more broods of chicks. It wasn't a brood of chicks I had in mind when I finished the house, it was the season: the coming of rain, the relentless southeasterly blowing through the skeletal framework, rinsing the wood of life and colour.

We were first-time nesters with no knowledge of house building. But we had to do something, so I suggested I hire a carpenter. We would be the carpenter's helpers, working and learning, with access to tools that we otherwise wouldn't have. The role of employer was a serious one and I approached it with gravity, seeking out carpenters and learning what they expected to get paid. I promised good wages, showed candidates the project, spoke of timelines and materials. People gave advice, showed interest, made suggestions. But in the way of small towns in winter, my options began to dwindle. The first candidate disappeared to Hawaii, the next to Mexico. A third candidate showed up a few times, never when expected. And the fourth candidate? There wasn't a fourth candidate. As the situation unfolded, I gazed at raw materials, seeing them only as problems to be overcome. But one problem didn't lie within the framework of the floathouse. That problem involved a different type of foundation.

As if an inner door had closed, my partner stopped speaking about the house. He passed no opinions, offered no explanation. He faded from the discussion like a forest creature, hidden by perfect stillness. Perhaps my ambitions for the floathouse were too high. Or the problems seemed insurmountable. For some reason I didn't ask and for some reason he didn't tell me. Whatever the issue, the consistency of our relationship was becoming granular. I sensed the onset of a gentle crumbling. We ate together, laughed together, visited our friends together. But in matters pertaining to the floathouse, and in matters I could sense, but not see, I was now alone.

I'm outside on the garden dock when the sky shivers, parting the curtain of snow to let the wind through. The house recoils as if slapped and I hear another noise, a slow creaking that gathers in intensity. When I realize what it is, I scramble backwards, tripping over plant pots and rainwater butts, reaching safety just as a foot of snow whooshes from a section of the roof. The floathouse bobs upward with sudden one-sided buoyancy. The other side of the house, the kitchen side, sinks lower. In an all-too-familiar sight, the apex of the roof points to ten o'clock.

In memory, the simple act of building was the most trying experience of my life. The work was complicated by features unique to the floathouse. The two longer sides of the house were bordered by water—no deck or dock; no place, other than a boat, on which to stand or prop a ladder; no way to retrieve the tools that inevitably dropped into the water; and of course, no electricity. I tied long lines to my thirteen-foot Boston Whaler, set a stepladder on the boat's twelve-inch-wide wooden bench and climbed three precarious steps, siding in hand. One at a time, I nailed the boards to the side of the house. But inevitably, as I pushed against the house, the tie-up lines stretched and the boat countered my action by drifting away, stranding me at full reach over the water, arms trembling under the weight of wood, stepladder wobbling beneath me on the boat's bench. In this position I'd have to reach for my hammer. And a nail. If I could get the first nail in, the rest would go easier. That first nail, however, was the toughest adversary, my house of cards tumbling at the slightest provocation.

Most annoying were the passing boats. A boat wake was all it took to knock the stepladder, and me, from the bench. If a boat went by, I'd let go of the board I was holding, climb down from the steps and wait for the wake to roll through. When calm was restored I'd replace the steps and mount them once more. Two or three boats in a row were enough to reduce me to tears.

As if the glissade of snow has uncovered a cache of words, the details of my friend's warning suddenly spring back to me: Floathouses up north, sinking in the snow, becoming lopsided, flipping over. "Flipping over." He said that. I close my eyes, unable to look. Then I run through the house from one side to the other. I have to move the boat away from the eaves. A fall of snow like the last will sink it where it's tied. And whatever else happens, I need my boat.

Piece by piece, the floathouse neared completion. I bought foam insulation and pine panelling, the lightest weight possible. I rescued old windows, sanded and repainted them. My friend Ike installed them, adding pretty trim. In a complex operation, real carpenters showed up for work (when they said they would) and installed custom windows in the loft—double paned and storm strong, each one as tall as me. My work as a kayak guide took the majority of my hours, but the floathouse claimed the rest. Every evening for weeks, I wielded a six-inch belt sander, smoothing rough-cut cedar dock planks until they blushed soft pink. My right shoulder seized, requiring physiotherapy to fix, but I was so hyped I barely cared. I sealed the cracks between each board and then added coat after coat of varnish, making a floor of the utmost beauty. Domesticity left me. The longer the daylight hours, the longer I worked. That summer I remember a single day off. Unable to function, or even look at the floathouse, I drove to Echachis, unfurled a sleeping bag and slept in the sun on the beach, not stirring until evening shadows laid cool hands on my face.

Despite my exhaustion, I began to feel strong. Inner strength, which had ebbed as I neglected my own life in support of my partner's, now crept into spaces that had recently grown hollow.

It's three in the morning and I'm fumbling with the lines of the boat, my fingers swollen and numb. I guide the boat away from the avalanche zone of the roof. I dig into the snow, retrieve an oar, and paddle to the safety of the garden dock, where I stare at the tip-tilted house, wishing for an outrigger, anything to add stability. Then I kneel in the boat and begin to bail, an act of obeisance to appease the storm gods. The blue dustpan flashes back and forth in the beam of my headlamp. I move from bow to stern, grimacing as snow water seeps through the gap between rain pants and boots. Water seeps into my sleeves, too. As I scoop the last snow from the boat, water pools in the dustpan. Tired and cold, I slump on the seat. On the dock, dimples form in the snow, growing into puddles and ponds. Water soaks my hair, dripping

into my eyes and trickling down my neck. The dustpan fills and a clear riv-
ulet spills over the blue rim. I stare for long minutes before I register what
I've been missing—water! The snow has changed to rain.

The floathouse was finished in 1997, except for one further measure
that remained to be put in place. It had to move. Simple for a floathouse, complex for a quietly crumbling relationship. But Stone Island
faced the storms and the floathouse was a target. Wave after wave,
gust after gust, the house heeled over and back, its heavy framework
creaking and twisting. One gust blew out the kitchen window—a
single "bang!" and it vanished. I looked through the open hole and
saw the frame of it floating by the rocks, far across the bay. A vortex
followed, stealing papers and loose objects and whirling them out of
the hole. As we nailed a board over the empty space, I knew I couldn't
put off leaving. It was a loaded decision, because I sensed I'd be leaving behind more than just an island. But anchorage was waiting in
faraway Maltby Slough, a time-sensitive offer I couldn't refuse. The
move would be a leap of faith and one I might have to take on my
own. I shook out my wings and wondered if they would lift me.

The rain is falling west-coast style: drenching, filling, flattening, eroding.
A second weight of snow thumps from the roof and splashes into the sea,
this time from the other side of the house. I grip the gunwales of the boat,
relieved to have moved it in time. And as I stare at the water level of my
house, my eyes blurred with rainwater, I see something miraculous—a
way to add floatation to the sides. The water-level fascia boards hide a
crawl space, which would allow for the insertion of beams—beams that
could extend outward, allowing for a stabilizing, walk-around dock. It
looks complicated, but I know it can be done. I laugh. Stability—achiev-
able after all! The wind is lightening, shifting to the southwest when I
stumble into the house, stripping off my soaked clothes. A joyous sense of
possibility stretches me like the sky.

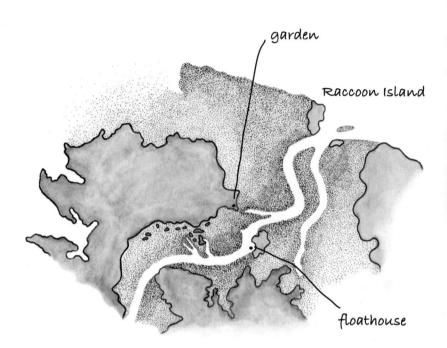

seal, like a mirage
you shimmer to sudden life
and likewise vanish

Wild Life

I've always been a capable spy. Drawn to inner landscapes, I drift easily into a private theatre of thoughts and images, lingering there while I gaze in parallel at the real world. But despite my watchfulness, important wildlife affairs still go unseen. And those very proceedings have the potential to affect my life. I learned this when I was nineteen and a bull orca rose out of the water directly in front of my kayak. I wasn't expecting whales and it was the first orca I'd ever seen. The four-foot dorsal fin made a noise like the flexing of sheet metal as it cut through the air toward me. My paddles whirled in full reverse, fuelled by a thumping heart and a surge of adrenaline, which didn't abate until the whale came abreast of me, his small all-seeing eye examining me before passing by.

In that moment I realized that the scope of my watchfulness needed to expand: I needed to become more observant, both of my immediate surroundings and of the larger view. I also needed to improve my ability to predict the general patterns of weather and wildlife—patterns that had the potential to affect the routines of life on the coast. With all the assurance of youth, I presumed these skills were not only something that would protect me, but also something I could master. It never occurred to me that animals could be just as fallible as humans. And that, despite my best intentions, my skills of observation could fail me.

My lessons in marine mammal behaviour began when I became a seal-pup nanny for the family who lived in Maltby Slough before me. The seal in question was a prematurely born harbour seal pup, found in a state of hypothermia and near drowning. He was raised by Mike and Cathie and their daughter, April, on the decks of their floathouse. And he was named Tutsup, the Tla-o-qui-aht word for urchin, a perfect *double entendre* for this orphan, who—when curious—could extend his whiskers until his nose bristled like a spiny sea urchin. Tutsup could also be shortened to Tootsie, or Toots, to match his babyish cries of *maaaa!* and the way he slurped his soother—an old wetsuit bootie—as if it were a thumb.

On the advice of marine biologists, Tutsup was tube-fed a life-saving fishy concoction and kept strictly away from the water. His white lanugo—a premature birth coat—nearly cost him his life, unprepared as he was for cold-water immersion. Had he been born further north, this coat would have kept him warm as he rested on an ice floe, but in the less frigid climes of the forty-ninth parallel, this coat is shed *in utero*, allowing full-term seal pups to be born swim-ready. For Tutsup, swimming wasn't an option until his swimming coat grew in, so he had to be kept dry. But keeping a baby seal dry and fed is a full-time job. And two days a week, when Tutsup's adoptive family were all at work, I drove up to Maltby Slough, donning my nanny cap as their floathouse came into view.

Single-handedly tube-feeding an obstinate infant seal is a handful of a job, prone to failure and mess. Nor did things improve when Tutsup grew old enough to digest the chunks of herring we were instructed to force-feed him. Should my forefinger not push the pieces far enough down his gullet, the whole disaster would be projected—cork-like—straight back at me. Through it all, I marvelled at the exquisite pinkness of his inner mouth, the muscular curl of his tongue, the tight round rolls of neck fat and the pathos of his hooting cries. Like a crawling child, he followed my movements, intent

on sucking the soft cotton of my pant legs. If allowed, he would wad the fabric into a slimy wet mass—anchoring me in place by the sheer force of his pull. As he grew older he began to lean over the dock and put his head in the water, blowing bubbles—and raspberries—for our mutual entertainment. And one day, when the time was right, he slipped into the water, lured by the magnetic pull of instinct.

Seamlessly, the water claimed him, erasing his domestic past and reshaping him as a wildling. Tutsup began to absent himself for longer and longer periods. He learned to catch his own fish, and stopped hooting and suckling, or seeking human companionship. Occasionally he hauled out to rest under the dock, where his loud breathing gave away his presence. Like a parent whose child has left home, part of me longed for Tutsup to keep our connection. But however bittersweet, I knew that what had happened was the best possible outcome. From time to time I saw him, either from my motorboat or from my kayak, and when I did, I couldn't help calling out to him, secretly wishing he missed me, hoping for a glimmer of recognition. Most times, though, his response was ambiguous—dark head sinking without any gesture beyond eye contact. I began to see the limitations of my role as a watcher, confined as I was to the world above water.

That feeling of limitation continued during the years I worked as a whale-watching guide. Daily, I studied the visual language of whale spouts—those spectral puffs of distilled breath, nuanced by wind, sky, the size of the whale, its distance, speed and many other factors. Trip after trip I tried to gauge how long a whale would remain submerged, how soon it would reappear, how it might behave once on the surface. My predictions became more reliable, despite the beautiful prerogative of whales, like seals, to conceal themselves by slipping away into the depths, leaving me longing to know what they did when lost from view.

But while it was rich in marine mammals, life on the water didn't preclude the observation of land animals. In fact, terrestrial animal behaviour gained a new dimension in my work as a kayak guide. Kayaking is a perfect environment for spying on animals. The boats travel close to shore, often observing the intertidal equivalent of cross-border traffic. This interface of land and sea is the domain of herons, ducks and shorebirds. It's also attractive to mink and raccoon. They can be seen foraging for small crabs, or sniffing the air before setting off on a swim, always with a destination in mind. Black bears, too, are drawn to the intertidal zone, endlessly turning over rocks in search of crabs. In some areas the clunking of boulders makes up a common, multi-dimensional aspect of the low-tide landscape.

Over the years these observations began to coalesce, melding into a strange combination of knowledge and instinct. But as with all areas of study, the more I learned, the more I wanted to know.

It was not just because of Tutsup that I took up swimming expeditions the summer after I moved to Maltby Slough. So many creatures used the channel as a transportation route that I thought it would be fun to do what they did, follow similar paths, map out my surroundings from their perspective. At low tide, the channel lent itself to exploration. I could zigzag upstream by swimming from the house to the mudflats on the far side, walking for about ten minutes, swimming across again and walking further. In this way I could reach the corner where the channel narrowed and curved out of sight—a high-traffic area for wildlife in the slough. Wolves often crossed here, noses and tails held high as they swam with remarkable speed. My own swimming was also speedy, on account of the frigid temperature and strong current. The constant feed of fresh water meant that the slough was always cold, even when water temperatures elsewhere warmed. The current was another matter, often dangerously strong depending on the tide. I chose my moments with care, not wanting to find myself stranded downstream, cold and wet and tired.

One glorious August afternoon, I headed out to swim and walk. Leaving home was the most challenging part of the adventure. The floathouse was tucked in the curve of a small bay and the ebbing current aimed straight at it, undercutting the shore of the island behind it before rebounding. The resultant swirl of water spread across the channel, bumping back into the main thrust of the ebb. It was the widest span I could choose to cross, and the most complicated. Added to this was my body's dubious ability to adjust to the icy baptism. Always a challenge, I would sit on the edge of the boat with my feet immersed, waiting for a small seed of courage to grow and blossom.

On this windless day, the tide was low, and small, airborne flocks of shorebirds banked and flashed their way along the water's edge, seeking sustenance for their journey south. The mudflats were bright with the carpet of moss-green algae that spreads and thickens throughout the summer—algae that is a nuisance when boating, but the fibrous cushioning of which felt good underfoot, protecting me from stray rocks and excess mud. For a change, I decided to walk downstream toward Browning Passage. I wanted to see how far I could make it without encountering any impassable, ankle-grabbing sections of mudflat. These were usually the low-lying places, where trickling water pooled and there was little eelgrass. I didn't get very far before wading back out and swimming downstream to avoid a quagmire. I couldn't cross back over to Aquila Island because the shoreline was steep and rocky there—clad with a horde of barnacles.

I swam for as long as I could stand the cold, then waded ashore and continued along my way.

As excursions go, it was a messy one. I began to resemble a swamp monster, strung with ribbons of eelgrass and smeared with mud. I gave up on my plan and decided instead to visit the cabin my neighbour was occupying in his capacity as a squatter. There was a garden there and I'd been offered a small plot of earth where I planted kale and potatoes. Without a water supply, gardening was more whimsical than practical, but I liked the idea of it. My neighbour was practising a very different kind of gardening—one we didn't discuss. But at this late date in the summer, he was nearing his harvest time, which may have explained his absence that day.

I climbed up the dark rocks—avoiding barnacles—and sat for a while, soaking up the warmth and the scent of woodbine honeysuckle. From this viewpoint I was able to see the stickiest areas of mudflat and think about the route home. Later, I wandered into the garden and examined withered stalks of potatoes and small, tough leaves of kale, hoping that no respectable gardener would ever see my handiwork. It wasn't until I was leaving that I noticed something different—large claw marks, slashed brightly across the pale bark of an alder tree, the orange flesh of the tree exposed and bleeding. The marks were new and they were clearly the work of a bear. My neighbour hadn't mentioned a bear to me, a fact that made me wonder just how new the marks were. *Hmm*, I thought, *time to head home.*

I pulled apart the wall of honeysuckle vines and peered out over the mudflats, searching for boulder-sized black shapes. Bears usually forage at shoreline, looking for crabs, or using their teeth to scrape barnacles from logs for a popcorn-like snack—extra crunchy. I took care in my search, squinting into the distance, shielding my eyes with both hands. Happily, there was no bear visible and I stepped lightly onto the mudflats. When, halfway there, a horsefly found me—buzzing and landing despite my slaps—I began to lose concentration and fortitude, in equal measure. Bears were generally avoidable, horseflies weren't. I strayed from my intended path and my feet became bogged down in the stickiest of the mud. I made such a perfect target that a second horsefly joined the fray, scenting a blood meal. My slaps doubled in number as I twisted and writhed, trying to escape the flies' cutting mouth parts. I longed for the swim home, to rid myself of mud and insects and grubby strands of eelgrass. Such distractions undermine even the best of safeguards.

Once I could see the boat I decided to swim for it, even though I was still upstream of my usual crossing point. I was warm from my efforts and the water itself would be warmer than before. The tide had turned, imbued with the heat of sunbaked mudflats as it flooded the bay. I splashed in, wallowing and sighing with relief, pulling low the brim of my hat to thwart the location-finding of malicious horseflies. I estimated my course to the floathouse, taking into account the sweeping arm of the tide. Then I swam quickly, hoping I wouldn't get too cold.

My boat's small white shape grew larger as I swam. It was an important target, one which I had no intention of overshooting. But I needed a bigger picture of my place within the channel, to see where the current was sweeping me. I treaded water, turning a circle and looking around. The dark head of a seal caught my interest as I turned, my vision blurring as salt water splashed into my eyes.

The seal was a few body lengths from my shoulder, heading the other way. Tutsup had often seemed spooked by the presence of swimming humans when he was little, but he had a dark head. Could it be him? Had he finally come to see me? Several years had passed since I'd last poked a herring down his throat. I couldn't be sure if that broad neck belonged to him. And the fur seemed extra dark. There was also something wrong with the shape of his head. It was long and flat and not very seal-like. Kicking hard to keep my place in the current, I tried to clear my eyes of salt water and get a better view. That was when I noticed the creature's ears. Harbour seals don't have visible ears.

The realization that I was swimming alongside a black bear had a similar effect on me as my early encounter with the bull orca. I shot across the channel without concern for the current or the temperature. Was the bear aware of me? I didn't know. Several times I shoulder checked, but thankfully the two black ears kept moving progressively toward the opposite shore. Later, I was surprised that so little of the bear's body showed above water, but at the time I thought nothing of it. With a surge of great energy, I hauled my flailing body over the gunwales of the boat and looked behind me again. By now, the bear had also finished swimming and was wading out of the water, eelgrass streaming from his haunches. I particularly enjoyed his choice of landing site, smirking at his arrival in the middle of the very quagmire I'd just escaped, where he sank into the mud even as he shook out his coat—water spraying brightly from his fur. From my position of safety, I began to laugh, the sound of my relief pealing out into the echoing open space. Two creatures swimming on a hot late-summer day, neither one of us plotting a careful course, our actions unguided by any sense of vigilance, or wisdom.

I peeled long strands of eelgrass from my legs and watched the bear's muddy progress. Despite the distance I felt sure I could see two horseflies circling his head.

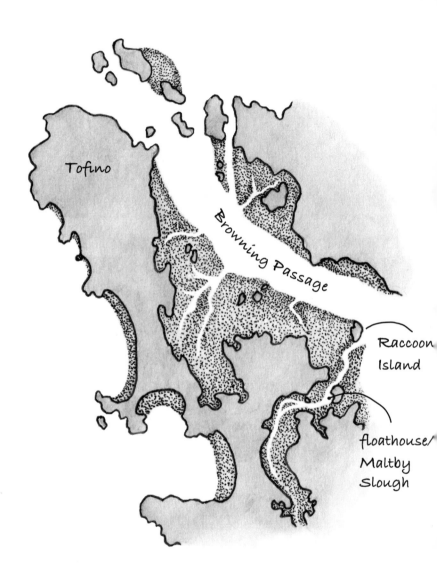

branch over green branch
concealing the heart, where truth
is written in rings

Breathless

There are only two occasions when I've been seriously ill with asthma: one was the winter of 1999 after my father died; the other was the spring of 2008 after my mother died. For practitioners of Chinese medicine, grief is the territory of the lung, making it unlikely that my twin visits to the hospital were coincidental. But a journey to hospital can be simple or complicated. One trip to the hospital felt, at times, as if it could be my last.

When I moved my floathouse to Maltby Slough in 1997, the experience was like stepping into air. It was further from town than I had yet lived and I had to negotiate winter conditions in Browning Passage—an exposed body of water over which waves and winds accelerate. Patterns of water flow in Clayoquot Sound are always complex, but here, deep water ebbs from the terminus of faraway Tofino Inlet, reaching an island-choked bottleneck at Tsapee Narrows, where it begins to boil and seethe. When it escapes, still churning, it spreads out into Browning Passage and is constrained on each side by an estuarine slow lane: acres of mudflat stretching out toward the Tofino peninsula on one side and Meares Island on the other. Thus flanked, the passage takes a dogleg route west toward Tofino, pausing briefly to mass and swirl around the Laddie Island rocks.

The mudflats are the trickiest part. For a small boat, the eelgrass-clad shallows can be crossed only at certain moments in the tide. Through them, an arterial network of small branching channels maintains the circulatory system of the mudflats and allows Maltby

Slough a river-like drainage into Browning Passage. At high tide, I could drive over most areas of the mudflats and take a reasonably direct route home. But at low tide, I had to follow one of the channels. About twenty feet wide, the channel led from Raccoon Island, near Tsapee Narrows, to Aquila Island, where my home was moored. Serpentine, it slithered through the mud, visible only at low tide. I could drive through it at low water, but at mid-tide the surrounding mudflats were covered with shallow water—meaning that if I strayed from the now-invisible channel, I would find myself suddenly ramming the mudflats. As I drove, I counted the seconds between each turn. I followed landmarks on fair days and compass bearings on foggy days. At night, my eyes slid along the blackened outline of the land, seeking the second highest knoll or the twinkling radio beacon near Radar Hill. If my landmarks failed, I could easily go aground. There was much to guard against.

Added to the challenges of my location, I was newly single after a seven-year relationship. The pain of this separation was somewhat mitigated by the allure of a fresh beginning. As well, I had the companionship of my large and entertaining dog, Sweetheart. And Maltby Slough itself played a part in my healing. I relished the sanctuary of my new location: the way Aquila Island protected me from the southeast gales, the total lack of boat traffic, the increased exposure to wildlife. I settled in, tackling the winter commutes, beachcombing and cutting my own firewood, and learning the number of candles it takes to survive the month of December (about three hundred).

Two years after moving to Maltby Slough, my father died. I was thirty years old and he died as I was driving to the airport to visit him in England. Because I lived so far from my parents, I hadn't fully perceived the volatility of his health. What I did understand was the sharp bite of regret at the way I had so blithely lived my life. Missed moments lay scattered around me like so much sand. Caught up in youth, and with an ocean to separate us, I hadn't sensed the ever-accelerating passage of time. It was as if I thought I could later gather up the grains and refill the hourglass. But death is the swiftest of teachers.

When I developed a cough, not long after I returned from my father's funeral, what surprised me was not the fact that I'd caught a virus, but how rapidly it became painful. Within a day I was incapacitated. Any movement made me breathless. My old blue inhaler sat next to the bed while I counted down the hours between doses. From time to time, I roused myself to drink tea and stoke the fire. Sweetheart was solicitous, taking the stairs beside me, her soft white head brushing my hand as I walked. Back in bed, I kept my breaths deep and even by concentrating on faraway objects. I observed the overlay of branch upon branch in the forest outside my window. And in those places where the branches were so thick as to obscure the depths of the forest, I was frustrated by my inability to see what the foliage concealed. It was a failure of the imagination, in the same way that I couldn't grasp my father's new state of being dead. As if it were a brick wall that separated us, I wondered if being able to perceive the heart of the forest—to see what lay on the other side of the branches—was an ability that would also allow me to comprehend my father's death.

I tried and failed to explore the idea through poetry while Sweetheart stretched across the foot of the bed, regarding me. Her understanding of death was obviously superior to mine, uncomplicated by the need for explanation. I'd once watched her resuscitate one of her offspring and marvelled at the insistent drive of her tongue into the pup's clogged airway. She'd become a first-time mother merely an hour before this and was taken aback by the puppies' arrival, but her response was everything it should have been—a miracle of instinct and body chemistry.

At suppertime I went down to the kitchen and heated some soup, but soon gave up eating and rested my elbows on the edge of the table, head hanging down, ribcage working like a squeezebox as I tried to catch my breath. I needed the inhaler, but it wasn't yet time to take it and I wanted to ration the dose until bedtime. The night loomed ahead of me and I sensed it was going to be long. Under the table, Sweetheart nudged my legs and I reached a hand down to rest it on her head. Later, I broke the evening's chores into small steps, most important of which was to feed the woodstove. The night was clear and cold, and frost already glittered on the moist wood of the dock. By the time I mounted the stairs with my candle, I was thinking of only one thing: the inhaler beside my bed. I would take the prescribed dose, fluff up the pillows and then, miraculously, fall asleep. Sleep would distract me from the pain in my chest and the medication would allow me to breathe. Tomorrow, I would go to the clinic and speak to a doctor. Everything would be better.

It must have been about twenty minutes after using the inhaler that Sweetheart got up from her blanket and came over to the head of the bed, shifting her weight from foot to foot as she gazed at me. I was waiting for the medication to take effect so that I could blow out the candle and go to sleep, but had felt no relief—yet. I considered going into town and sleeping at a friend's house, in case my breathing worsened. That way I'd be able to ask for help if I needed it. But it was after ten o'clock on a January night. It was dark and bitterly cold. Even the boat's tie-up lines would have lost their pliancy and be stiff with frost. I leaned against the pillows and tried to reframe the night as an opportunity to heal. As strategies go, it was well-intentioned, but ineffective. Sweetheart's unwavering gaze intensified, but against my thirst for air her concern seemed external—a faraway thing.

Just then, a new noise made its way into my world: the deep-deeper two-tone boom of the foghorn, resounding from the lighthouse at Lennard Island. On stormy winter nights, the foghorn relayed the sheer inability of the lighthouse keepers to see anything except rain, waves and windborne spray. But on a calm, clear night, a night such as this one, the message was simple: fog had formed offshore. It wouldn't be long before it came slinking over the Tofino peninsula into Maltby Slough. And when that happened, my options would be limited. I sat up and took notice. I don't mind driving a boat at night. And I don't mind driving a boat in the fog. But driving in fog and darkness, both, was something I'd chosen to stop doing.

This decision came about during a particularly nail-biting drive home. I'd left the Tofino Harbour under clear night skies and headed east to the green buoy in Browning Passage. A midway point of sorts, the buoy was the furthest I could go on a single bearing, and its Christmas-green reflective tape was easy to see. At the green buoy I would change bearings and head southeast toward Raccoon Island.

Most nights I could see my landmarks with relative ease, driving without the compass, but on this night, after leaving the green buoy I drove straight into a swath of fog. Surprised, I made an about-face turn and drove back out the way I'd come. Sure enough, I could see that the fog was a mere tendril, pressed against the surface of the water, entirely unconnected to any parent cloud. The fog covered only the area of water I needed to cross and it was barely higher than my head. But, as if sensing my presence, it stretched out to welcome me. Its white fingers reached behind me, obscuring the green buoy from my line of sight. In that swift moment, my compass bearing became obsolete; I no longer had the point of origin from which to draw the bearing. Starting in the wrong place could mean overshooting Raccoon Island and ending up further east, in Tsapee Narrows. I had to guess at a bearing, so I aimed further west. That way I would only run into the soft sand of the mudflats if I were wrong. I could then use the perimeter of the mudflats as a guide. In the way of all dealings with fog-blindness, a conflict arose between my inner and outer compasses, my instincts doing battle with the smug accuracy of the compass. The headlamp illuminated the compass, but prevented me seeing anything else. I chewed my lip, doubting myself every second of the way forward. When I finally sighted the edge of the mudflat, I abandoned the compass and turned off the headlamp to regain vision. Even the chimerical, vanishing line of low-tide mud was an improvement on the nihilism of the fog. It was a tense journey. And as I worked my way to Raccoon Island, I vowed to avoid a repeat experience.

But now, the foghorn's advanced warning was giving me a chance to get to town while the sky was clear. And I knew I shouldn't wait for my breathing and the visibility to worsen. In fog and darkness, even the Coast Guard would have trouble navigating the channel to Maltby Slough. I shook off my cloak of self-absorption and swung my legs over the edge of the bed. Motion by slow motion, I packed a drybag of essentials and changed into warm clothing. At the bottom of the stairs, I paused to breathe and to lift the heavy floater jacket from its hook. I pulled on boots, one at a time, with a rest in between. Lastly, I put on a red cashmere scarf—a present from my mother— and a toque—a pound-weight of Cowichan wool, knitted by Tla-o-qui-aht elder Mary Hayes.

Stepping into the night air, I felt my windpipe seize against the cold. But the plan was underway and there was no room for self-doubt. I executed each action in sequence and buried my nose and mouth in the folds of the scarf, chest heaving, as I approached the boat. Sure enough, the tie-up lines were stiff and solid. I sat down on the railing as I worked the lines loose, fingers burning with cold. I never wear gloves before leaving a dock, because they always get wet. Not until a boat ride is underway do gloves become an option. While I fiddled with the lines, I examined the forty-horse outboard. It tended to be a fair-weather motor, preferring summer climes to winter's extremes of rain or cold. A furring of hoar frost on the cover hinted at trouble ahead and I pumped the gas line with extra care, making the bulb as firm as possible. I set the choke and grasped the pull cord. But pull cords require an explosive effort on the part of the puller, one that I didn't fully anticipate. Air left my chest in a whoosh. For a moment, I blacked out.

In the time lapse between falling and recovering, I drifted, seeing my father hop from foot to foot in the sweaty night air outside Trinidad's Piarco Airport, calling my name in staccato bursts, his forehead tight with anticipation. I was twelve and we'd been apart for three months. When he saw me, his face lit up in a trademark expression of joy, a look that never failed to bring out my fiercest love for him. The sensation ran through me in a short euphoric burst, flooding me with the energy I needed to regain air. After a minute or two I was able to sit up, wheezing, and prepare to depart. Sweetheart hopped onto the bow, her favourite spot in the boat. But as my hand reached for the tie-up line, the motor suddenly sputtered and no amount of fiddling could keep it going.

A perfect silence followed, almost echoing in the extreme calm of the bay. One likelihood was that the carburetors had frozen, but there was also a chance that the motor was flooded. If so, I would need to leave it alone for a few minutes and let the excess gas evaporate. I sat on the homemade yellow cedar bench, staring at cold faraway stars, one hand on Sweetheart's head, the other gliding over the varnished wood surface. Through the scarf, I took a series of tight breaths and stood up to restart the motor. This time I braced myself, expecting the effort. I managed three pulls and fell backwards once again. The stars blurred. I cried out in frustration. Doubt was taking hold of me: I doubted my ability to start the motor. I doubted my ability to make it to town. I doubted if I could survive the night. Sweetheart began to lick my face. I wondered if I resembled her dying pup and if she planned to lick me back to life. The thought made me sit up, holding onto her. She gave a low "wuf," her breath forming bright clouds between us. I turned around and tried the motor again, this time managing four pulls. Then I sank onto my knees, swaying and heaving for air.

The second-last time I said goodbye to my father, I told him I loved him. I thanked him for his restraint—the times he'd withheld criticism, the things he could've said, but didn't. I thanked him for keeping the peace while I warred with adolescence; for building the bridges that led me back home. I said this over a cup of tea, after a lunch of soup and bread. I said it when we were alone, just him and me. We sat in the quiet kitchen and let our eyes say everything else. We were in the front hall when my mother arrived with the car. I hugged him, not knowing if I would see him again, missing him already. I held his hands, and then bolted outside, the door a dam against my tears. But as we drove away, I saw movement in the rear-view mirror. Dad had hobbled to the road to wave until I disappeared. I'd shut the door in his face, not offering him my arm, or helping him turn the stiff door handle. In the rearview mirror, his eyes were large with pain, his forehead lined. I saw him vanishing, saw us both vanishing—each from the other's life. Like an accordion my emotions opened up, the bellows sucking air.

My hands gripped the textured fibreglass floor of the boat; my ribs flailed. I gulped and heaved. When I saw exhaust fumes misting the dark air, I lurched forward and grabbed the tiller handle, desperate to keep the motor running. I hauled myself onto the bench, letting go the last tie-up line and pulling away from the house without even the energy to look back. The boat rose up onto a plane and left the bay, carving through the bends of the channel on the way to Raccoon Island. Visibility was still good and I could see the channel clearly. And frigid as it was, the rushing air seemed to help me breathe. As we got closer to Tofino I found my shoulders loosening. I relaxed further, letting the ride prime me for the final stretch of the journey, up the hill by foot to the hospital.

Unlike the sudden collapses caused by pull-starting the motor, walking uphill took my air away with greater stealth. Beginning at the boat ramp, I noticed the effort and stopped often to rest. Later, at the steepest part of the hill, a tunnel began to form in my vision, blacking out peripheral distractions. By the time I stood outside the hospital door to ring the bell, I was viewing the world as if through a periscope. I remember making a bed of my floater coat for Sweetheart and asking her to wait outside. I remember the heaviness of the double doors and I remember gesturing to my chest, unable to speak. I remember the kindness in nurse Chris Curley's eyes as she led me inside, her face the only bright shape in my vision.

That night in hospital, I received medication and compassion, enough that breathlessness and grief ebbed from me. I leaned against white pillows, wanting to sleep, not knowing if I could. With only walls to observe, my mind emptied, matching the view. The nurses checked on Sweetheart and found her wandering, listening for my voice. Somehow she located my room and stopped outside the window, curling into a soft ball, not moving until I was allowed to see her in the morning. When I did, she howled loud and long in her always-vocal way, bringing onlookers to the door. I coughed and wheezed and laughed. She was pleased to see me. But she also needed breakfast. Yesterday was out of our hands, but today was another story. Life could be simple that way.

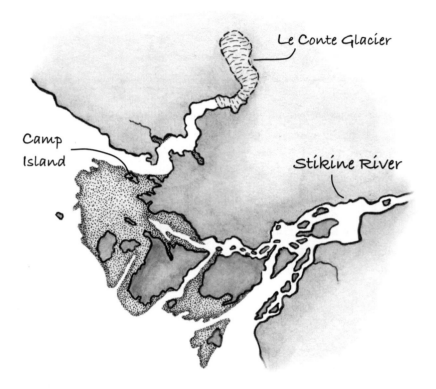

clouds mass on the peaks
darkening snow-streaked mountains
I dream of warm skin

The Colour of Time

An army is bearing down on me. I am trying to make a run for it, but the soldiers advance without pause, carried by the tide, their turquoise armour gleaming. Did Salvador Dali paint me into this scene? No, this is not a painting; and no, those are not soldiers, they are icebergs. But like Dali's famous clocks, the chunks of ice are melting with every minute. Their bizarre shapes lure my eyes. They are dogs, seals, birds, hands—even the parted legs of a synchronized swimmer, toes pointing skyward. The water is a deep, frigid green—impossibly smooth—interrupted only by these outlandish shapes.

Today is typical of southeast Alaska, I'm told. I can almost make out the horizon, but only because is has been brought nearer—everything else blotted out by the softest swath of grey. It is not raining, but the air is moist and thick. In this phantom sky, every nearby object pulses with colour and shape, which is why these chunks of ice command my attention completely. They pockmark every degree of the view, many of them stranded on the prairie-like expanse of mudflat that stretches from the main shoreline out to Camp Island, at the mouth of LeConte Bay.

∽

The day before, when Cindi and Dave and I had left the Stikine River and paddled northward up the coast toward Petersburg, we were nearly stranded on this vast mudflat—which would have been embarrassing for a trio of kayak guides like ourselves. Alaska was a first for me, but my friends were familiar with the coastline, having spent a winter on Baranof Island. They knew that the tidal range could be as much as twenty-four feet, about the height of an average two-storey house. Imagine a fjord becoming twenty feet shallower in the space of six hours. Imagine, then, the speed at which the water is pulled away. It was vanishing from underneath us as we travelled, getting shallower with every desperate paddle stroke. At one point we looked down through the water to see the paw prints of several wolves on the mud beneath us. Mixed among them were the hoofprints of two ungulates, probably deer. I reached my hand into the cold ocean and tried to touch them, but they were just beyond arm's length. This was a good sign; it meant we still had sufficient water depth. Not much, but some. With evening approaching, being stranded on the mud for six hours or more did not appeal, especially with the frigid gusts of wind that were rushing at us from the glacier. Our paddle strokes became ever quicker. I found myself sucking in my breath—as if without the excess weight of air, I could become lighter and my boat float higher.

Somehow we made it, setting our tents on Camp Island near the snout of the LeConte Glacier. Short of water, we collected pieces of glacial ice to melt. The melting took a surprisingly long time. I wondered how many years of accretion each minute represented. Having been subjected to intense pressure, glacial ice is much denser than regular ice. That density is apparent in the deep, tremendous colour. From a distance I saw the colour as turquoise. Under closer observation, the heart of the colour could have been cyan, but the colour itself seemed unreachable, obscured by layers of glass-like ice, always just one layer away from being discoverable. After further consideration, I realized what should have been obvious right away: that glacial ice falls into a category of its own; it reflects the colour of time, not of pigment.

After dinner that evening, we walked out onto the muddy low-tide land. It was surreal to be examining icebergs on foot this way, but there they were, newly birthed, already out of sight of the glacier and now abandoned by the retreating water. They rested, not like soldiers, but like a crop of strange jewels, deposited willy-nilly, through which we wandered, looking, touching, admiring... One chunk of ice had a slight depression, filled with a puddle of water. I couldn't resist tasting it. How decadent to drink this! Then—the novice in the group—I choked on salt and was reminded that the mudflat had been ocean just hours before.

In the end we were driven back to camp by the cold. That night, the wind howled down off the glacier, building slowly and battering the thin walls of our tents. Buried in my sleeping bag, the cold still found me. Collapsing bergs thundered explosively, punctuating my dreams and waking me with moments of alarm. I began to fret about the weather.

∽

The next day, afloat on the thick green water, we are racing across a fairway of strange, frozen creatures. With the extreme, negative tide, there is only one route—a narrow channel to the northwest of Camp Island, where the green water is now pouring at five nautical miles per hour, or more. And with the water comes the ice. Fresh water that has travelled for millennia on land is succumbing to the salt of the ocean. The bergs are sailing out into Frederick Sound to meet their fate, becoming smaller and smaller along the way.

I am in my kayak, trying to cross the fast-moving water, but I feel like a squirrel dodging cars on a highway. The idea of a collision is nasty. I already know how cold the water is. I can feel it through the soft skin of the folding Feathercraft kayak. And I have already seen what can happen when an iceberg collapses. I have watched from shore, alerted by the screams of the gulls and the ear-filling boom that resounds across the wide-open space. I have watched the resulting waves pound the beach, hundreds of yards from the source, and I have picked up small pieces of glacial ice and felt their weight—not something to be trifled with.

In this surreal, Dali-esque moment, I am awash with thoughts of evolution. My body has not evolved in any way to meet the challenges of this environment. If an iceberg collides with my boat and I am submerged, my gasping, hyperventilating lungs will likely fill with water. I've experienced cold shock response before, so I know what it's like. I think of the birds and animals that are miraculously able to live in this water. Their ability to survive is humbling.

As if in response to my thoughts, an ice floe startles me, zooming by replete with a resting seal. Insulating blubber aside, seals' superior swimming ability gives them much less to fear from collapsing ice. They can slip between worlds with ease. The seal is swept out of sight and another one sails past, also on an ice floe. The procession is on. As I paddle and dodge each berg, panting and sweating, the reclining seals observe me like Cleopatra from her royal barge. Each one of them is a masterpiece of evolution. And me? I am such a novice in this environment. I feel separated from the seals by millennia.

Even when we have finally crossed over to the mainland, icebergs still dot our route. The tide is low and there they are, littering the steep, rocky shoreline, some tilted at rakish angles, some with holes right through them—perfect frames for the lush Alaskan rainforest behind them.

Gradually, my eyes wander upward to the steepest tree-clad coastline I have ever seen. And as I ponder the ability of trees to grow so tall on vertical granite, the ice gradually disappears behind me, while the cloud wraps itself more closely around my boat. Nature's palette is reduced to greys and greens. Even the cliffs fade in and out of view. The first raindrops materialize from the heavy air and I look behind me for one last glimpse of ice. There is nothing. Not even a horizon. I feel like an audience member, still sitting in my chair after the curtain has closed on a memorable performance.

But the performance isn't over and it won't be over any time soon. The glacier has been pushing ice into Frederick Sound for millennia without respite. The earth turns, the glacier grinds, the tides sweep back and forth across the mudflat. A lifetime is a meaningless measuring stick. From my seat in the kayak, with the cloud closing around me, the notion of time is overwhelming. My sense of it grows and grows, while my place within it diminishes, vanishing along with the Alaskan skyline.

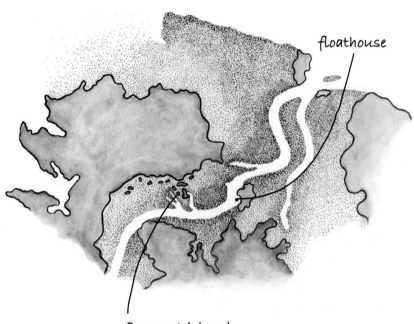

floathouse

Compost Island

wolf, a dappled ghost
you glide through tree-shadowed sand
lay tracks in my mind

Fair Game

"The hatred has religious roots: the wolf was the Devil in disguise. And it has secular roots: wolves killed stock and made men poor. At a more general level it had to do, historically, with feelings about wilderness. What men said about one, they usually meant about the other. To celebrate wilderness was to celebrate the wolf; to want an end to wilderness and all it stood for was to want the wolf's head."

Of Wolves and Men by Barry Holstun Lopez

It's hard to keep your sense of humour when you're running away from a wild animal on a wet, stormy winter evening. More than that, it's hard to hang onto your sense of self. That day in January 1999, I went from being a witness of nature to being a full-fledged participant. My previously comfortable relationship to the wild underwent a paradigm shift.

Before that day I wouldn't have thought I harboured any illusions about the wildlife in Clayoquot Sound, especially not about the wolves. "The wolves wouldn't confront me," I told people. "But I never let my dog anywhere near them; they would attack her, maybe kill her."

Over the years I have seen a lot of wolves—one of the privileges of a lifestyle that can otherwise be considered basic—even primitive. And while life on a floathouse isn't push-button—there is firewood to cut, drinking water to carry, a composting toilet to attend to, storms to endure, open-boat travel in all conditions—it is always rewarding for those with an interest in wild places.

In Maltby Slough, bald eagles nested close by; river otters swam past in gregarious troupes, chattering to one another, blowing bubbles under the floathouse; baby harbour seals hooted for their mothers with heart-rending pleas, while the adults—slick and silver—sometimes leaped out of the water in the light of the full moon. My appreciation was enhanced by the fact that these animals seemed to completely ignore me. My floating home and I merged with their landscape and there was harmony, it seemed. I assumed the voyeur's role with gravity, observed and enjoyed many moments, but the pinnacle of that enjoyment came not long after I'd first moved to Maltby Slough, the first day I saw the wolves.

I wrote about them at the time, describing how, at low tide, six wolves had spent two hours on the mudflats outside my house, playing with one another. It had been a beautiful morning, the liquid cry of a loon spreading across the low-tide landscape, echoing slightly in the quiet, wide-open space. Light from the rising sun glowed warm and yellow. And into this scene had trotted a wolf. Just like that, casually.

Clamping the binoculars to my eye sockets so tightly that they initially fogged up, I could see that it was truly a wolf, not a dog: tall and grey, with a moon-pale face and a reddish tinge behind the ears. Slim, but muscular, the understated power in its hind legs was apparent as it trotted, or rather, floated, across the beach.

Within twenty minutes four more wolves had arrived and together they played in the sun, running down the mudflats, unconcerned by the openness. They swam across the channel, then swam back again. They seemed to be waiting for something. Eventually a much larger wolf appeared. The younger wolves then laid an ambush for him and I watched as they squirmed with suspense and gave the game away

by pouncing too soon, smothering him with their enthusiasm. One young wolf observed a seal in the water and followed it as it swam slowly in the direction of my house, the seal observing the wolf with an equivalent amount of curiosity. They were only sixty feet away from me when the wolf realized that the rest of the clan had left and that he'd better rush to catch up with them. At the time, my final paragraph was imbued with awe. I wrote: "They melted into the shadows of the forest that morning, in the place where, not long ago, I had seen a bear. And they faded so sublimely that it's no wonder they seem mythical." As an introduction to living alone in Maltby Slough, it wasn't a bad place to begin.

Since that time, I have seen the wolves on many occasions. Once, at an extremely low tide, two of them squelched down to the water's edge by the house, barely fifteen feet from me as I squatted, motionless, on the doorsill. Other times they have appeared to me audibly as mournful songs in the moonlight. The winter before I first saw the wolves, a nearby family lost a dog to marauding wolves. Their other dog survived, but was badly hurt. Then, in the spring of that year, my neighbour's dog was attacked by a wolf.

The dog, Star, had been roaming the island behind my float-house. A small dog of blue heeler and pit bull parentage, she had spent the better part of that morning barking in the forest, the wilderness equivalent of announcing, "here I am!" or "free hot-dogs!" over a loudspeaker at a ball game. I had already shouted into the bush in the hopes of calling her or quieting her, but that hadn't worked. When I heard a loud scuffle, I presumed she was chasing something, but it didn't take long to realize that, in fact, something was chasing her. Fortunately she maintained good survival instincts and I was already preparing the boat when she barrelled out onto the shore with a young-looking wolf biting the scruff of her neck.

The two of them screeched to a halt when I stood up in the boat and yelled. Star then managed to scuttle to the water's edge, a bare ten feet from me. For almost thirty seconds the attacking wolf stood, hesitating, yellow eyes flicking back and forth between Star and me. Then my own dog spoke. It wasn't a loud bark, but it was deep and intent, clearly a warning. Standing up on the dock, Sweetheart was larger than the wolf, a fact that seemed to tip the scales of decision. The wolf retreated, but reluctantly, looking back often as I pushed the boat to the shore and picked up its trembling domestic cousin.

Apart from a few scratches and a coating of wolf saliva on her shoulders and haunches, Star was remarkably unscathed. As I examined her, I kept an eye on the forest, following the noise of the wolf as it crashed through dense salal. The tide was low enough for the wolf to leave the way it had come, across the mudflats to the main shoreline. After it crossed over, I continued watching, still waiting to see if other wolves were involved. Sure enough. Ten minutes later, the second wolf stole across the mud, furtive and quick, like a curl of smoke.

They say it is a technique the wolves have: only one animal reveals itself at first. This lessens the threat, makes a dog feel bold, inquisitive, more likely to approach the wolf. This way the other wolves do not have to stray too far from cover. Once lured to the forest, the dog does not stand a chance if there is an entire pack waiting. A friend once observed two wolves interacting with several river otters across the bay near here. The otters easily escaped into the water, after which nine more wolves filed out of the forest and continued travelling along the shoreline.

Do wolves differentiate dogs from other prey animals—seek them out for some kind of vengeance? The matter is often thought to be an issue of rivalry or dominance. It does appear that domestic dogs trigger a definite reaction among wolves, but in *Interactions of Wolves and Dogs in Minnesota*, a study by Steven H. Fritts and William J. Paul, it was also discovered that in fourteen out of nineteen cases, the dogs were partially or fully eaten, suggesting physical need. Something else sets the behaviour apart, because the study also notes that:

> While preying on dogs, wolves displayed a lack of fear of humans and buildings that is otherwise unknown except when they are diseased, disabled or preying on deer. In several incidents investigated, wolves evidently focused their attention on dogs so intently that they were almost oblivious to buildings and humans. Most wolf attacks on dogs occurred within the property owner's yard and, with only two exceptions, within a hundred metres of the owner's house. In one

case, a wolf attacked a dog near the doorstep and would not retreat until beaten with a shovel. This incident occurred after the owner had recently lost another dog and neighbours had, allegedly, lost two dogs. Four fatal interactions involved dogs chained to a residence or a doghouse. In those instances, the dog's collar was broken and the dog was carried away. In one case the doghouse was dragged into the adjacent woods with the dog carcass.

Perhaps, to adopt the wilderness metaphor of Barry Lopez, by attacking tame dogs, the wolves are making a statement, casting their vote in favour of continued wilderness.

I knew that wolves often attacked dogs, and I equated the rivalry to that of human street gangs—found it normal. Domestic dogfights are violent, too. But previously, wolves had always run away from me, never toward me. I didn't expect that they would overcome their fear of humans to get to a dog; that I would come between them, become the protector of my dog and thereby her reluctant proxy in the rivalry. I had yet to discover that just because I don't go looking for trouble, doesn't mean that trouble won't find me, and that if I slip up and make myself vulnerable then I am nothing other than fair game. Retrospectively, my earlier easy confidence in the bush was naïve—ridiculous. Is there a single creature that does not constantly fear for its life? How privileged I must be to sleep without fear, eat without fear, play without fear.

It was rainy and windy, that day in January, two years after I had first seen the wolves. I was on the mudflats, cutting firewood with the chainsaw, about half a kilometre from the floathouse. Because it was low tide, I had paddled there by canoe, unable to take the motorboat through the now-shallow channels. It was late afternoon, a poor time of day to have embarked on such a project.

Unfortunately the log was resting on the divide between firm sand and sticky mud. When I'd hauled the canoe up to the log, I'd had to pull each foot from the mud with my hands. And now each round of firewood was going to have to be carried across that mud, up the rocks of the nearest islet. That way I could come back for the wood with the motorboat when the water was deeper. The islet is a short distance from the main shoreline, but at low tide the mudflats connect them. It was just after I had carried up the sixth round that I noticed Sweetheart's odd behaviour: she was standing by the log, staring fixedly at the main shoreline. I followed her gaze and saw a large wolf trotting toward us over the mud.

My heart sank. The familiar grey fur blended well with the rest of the picture: the mud and the rain and the dimming light. I might not have seen the wolf without the sandy-red tint around its neck. Unlike mine, the wolf's feet moved easily over the mud, and they moved with confidence, purpose. This wolf was different from those I usually saw; it was more substantial—an easy match, visually, for Sweetheart's eighty-five pounds.

I considered firing up the chainsaw to see if it would frighten the wolf, but in reality the sound of the saw had probably drawn attention to us in the first place. I only had a limited period of time in which to leave, and really, that was what I had to do: remove the attraction; get my dog out of there. I didn't have time to play around with saws; I grabbed the canoe with one hand and the dog with the other. Miraculously my feet didn't stick in the mud this time and we moved smoothly, calmly down to the water.

The wolf was still approaching. The distance was closing. I pushed off, into the shallow water, but at that instant a gust of wind caught the canoe broadside and swept us into even shallower water. The canoe swished aground. This was silly. The wolf could trot through the water more swiftly than I could paddle.

I sighed. I would be a poor second in a fight and I didn't want the situation to reach that point. I stood up in the canoe and yelled, raising the paddle over my head to appear large and threatening. I stared at the wolf. His pace slowed. Then I stepped out of the canoe, turned my back to the wolf and started wading, towing the canoe behind me, Sweetheart standing up in it, motionless, staring at the wolf. By the time I reached a small sandbar, the wolf realized that the window of opportunity had slipped away and he stopped.

I waded on, the wind throwing handfuls of rain into my face, muddy water sluicing down my gumboots, my breath coming heavily even though I was keeping my pace deliberately moderate: what if the rest of the pack decided to venture out? I would need more energy. My thoughts narrowed to a tunnel that saw the quickest route home, the behaviour of the wolf, the possible approach of other wolves. I waded, tried paddling, then waded some more. Not until I was half a kilometre from the floathouse was I able to paddle across the channel and tie up the canoe. The trip had taken about twenty-five minutes. In all that time Sweetheart had never moved.

When we got out onto the dock she continued her vigil, sitting in the rain, staring, as if by having turned around to look at the wolf, she had somehow transformed into the legendary pillar of salt. I dried her off and locked her in the house. It was getting late and the tide was rising. I had to go back for the chainsaw or it would soon be submerged. My still-shaking hands pulled the cord of the outboard motor and I took the motorboat back across the water, searching the shoreline for the wolf—although, whether it was there or not, I still had to retrieve the saw. The flooding tide gave just enough depth to allow the motor clearance over the eelgrass beds. I beached the boat and squelched up to the saw, pausing to examine the line of wolf tracks. As expected, there was no deviation in the track line, no hesitation or second thought; the wolf had taken the shortest route possible to reach us—a straight line. It was pitch black when I got home the second time. There was mud all over everything and I was soaked and stiff with exhaustion. My expedition had been successful but for a few rounds of firewood. I had been fortunate to come out of such an important lesson unscathed.

In the week leading up to this adventure, four dogs had been killed by wolves in the nearby village of Ucluelet. Fear and resentment had boiled over quickly. There were instant cries for the wolves to be "deported." In a letter to the local newspaper, the owner of one of the dead dogs wrote: "I am in the midst of taking appropriate steps to protect our residents, my new pup and myself. I will not for one second hesitate to shoot any or all of these wolves when they return, and they will." The hysteria had started.

I sat at home and pondered my own reactions. I was never worried about the wolf being interested in me, but I knew I would have been unable to break up a fight between him and the dog—except maybe with the chainsaw or the axe. When I broke my thoughts down further I realized that I was uneasy about the fact that my presence had become insignificant to the wolf in light of the greater attractant, the dog. The canids were ignoring the *Homo sapiens*. In my arrogant human way, it shook me that the wolf had been so bold. It also bothered me that the wolf, or wolves, had been watching me without my knowledge, spying on me, ironically, just as I have spied on them: Are they watching me right now? I wondered. If so, where are they? Will I ever feel comfortable in the bush now?

Added to this was the nocturnal howling that had started going on, loud and long, just a stone's throw away, on the island behind the house. It was as if they were taunting me. "Go away and leave us alone!" I shouted one night, as their eerie songs penetrated my dreaming and my waking. On one of those nights, clear as a bell, I could see why humans fear wolves, why they have persecuted them, made them out as wicked beasts. I could do that too. I could cry for the deportation of the wolves; I could get a rifle...

But to live out here, I have to live with wildlife, not against it; I have to experience the beauty and the violence; I have to be part of the circle—accept that at some moments, when the wheel turns, my position will be lowlier than that of others. I have to take care, guard my territory and myself, just like the rest of the animals do—every minute, every second. After all, there really is no big bad wolf; there is only life.

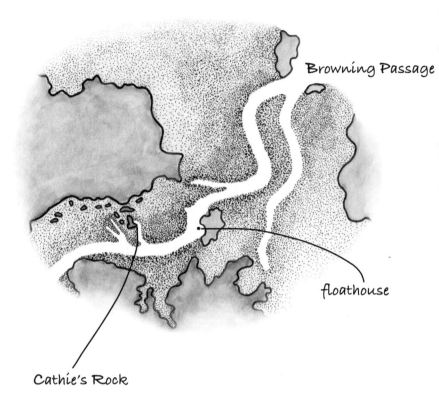

Browning Passage

floathouse

Cathie's Rock

this closeness—my breath
in your hair, my arms your shield
and I am newborn

Letting Go

In the winter of 2003, while visiting my mother in England, I dreamed I was standing on a pebble beach at Echachis Island. Heavy grey waves sucked rockslides down the seething beach and out to sea. The waves surged back again, gulping at the shoreline with wolfish hunger. The edge began to fall away as I stood there. I should have stepped back, but in the way of dreams, my friend Miriam appeared at my shoulder and began explaining how life would be once my baby was born. She didn't notice the waves. I woke from the dream in a state of mild terror, turning on the light and digging through my suitcase for my date book. Bleary-eyed, I began counting backwards through the days, realizing that my dream's message was, in fact, relevant.

The reason I could be expecting a baby had to do with my new situation, which had begun several years after I'd moved to Maltby Slough. One day I drove into the harbour on my way to town, in my little white Boston Whaler with my large white dog at the bow, nose into the wind, fluffy tail held high. Cutting in front of my boat came another white Boston Whaler, this one with a male driver and a black dog at the bow, nose into the wind, tail held high. *Seriously?* I grumbled. *Who's that?*

Maltby Slough had been a personal haven for several years. But change, it seemed, was underway. It wasn't long before I met the Boston Whaler's owner and his loyal dog, Relic. Marcel was a diver and fellow water dweller. And for the next four years we commuted by boat between each other's floathouses—each in a different inlet. But on a spring day in 2003, we combined households, filling the new storage boxes I'd built and rearranging my space—six hundred square feet, all told. I wondered how we would fit, in more than one sense of the phrase. The day after my dream, I called Marcel from England to share the unexpected news that I was pregnant. As international phone calls go, it was a quiet one.

The heart is a roomy place, given to expansion. My feelings for my wild home didn't have to shrink to accommodate a partner and a child. Inversely, they seemed boundless in their elasticity. Before having a child, I didn't sigh over baby photos and coo at the cuteness of them. Even in my thirties, my biological clock didn't send messages of alarm. When Marcel and I finally moved in together, it wasn't with the aim of becoming parents; more, it was an expression of trust, in each other and in the future. So when I discovered I was pregnant at thirty-five, I was thankful—not only for the biological stretching of skin, muscle, ligament—but also for the way my psyche expanded to include such fierce maternal love and protectiveness. What I didn't expect, however, was the way those protective arms could become restraints.

It started gently, with the distress I felt when my daughter, Toby, cried. It pained me to think she could be unhappy. The feeling took flight when I picked up a newspaper and saw photos of the Russian hostage crisis: 331 people killed by Chechen rebels, 186 of them children. It was early September 2004. Sunlight warmed the house but horror ran through me. Dead children! This was monstrous! It didn't matter if the children were mine or not. My job was to protect them and already I was failing. What was war but humans killing each other's children? That week we were staying at a friend's house on land, but in memory I was living in a war zone.

The future became a suddenly bleak place. Over the phone, my mother referred to the "terrible responsibility" of motherhood. Now

I could see what she meant. My mind reeled with the seemingly impossible mission of delivering a child safely to adulthood. Even breast milk is now laced with PCBs and other toxins. Was I poisoning my baby as I fed her? Or was I inoculating her against an already poisoned world?

But it was the dominant aspect of the floathouse—the water—that became my biggest adversary. In Maltby Slough, the ebb and flow of the tide created a constant water flow under my house. It was like living on a river. When I looked overboard from my house, I saw dark water, moving fast—twenty feet deep, but seemingly bottomless. Once, my cellphone accidentally slipped in. I watched its glowing green digits for about five seconds. After that, nothing.

We took Toby home on a glorious early autumn day, the kind that makes you feel as if the best of summer has only just arrived. We all enjoyed the boat ride home, the low-slanting sun so warm on our faces, me gripping my precious cargo through the cotton sling. At home, I carried Toby out of the boat and stepped from the garden dock to the floathouse, a distance of about two feet. When I looked down, dark water swirled beneath me, nothing reflected in it, nothing revealed by it. I thought of the baby—*my* baby—falling, sinking, vanishing beneath that wordless surface. The water showed me how quickly an infant could be destroyed. *About five seconds. After that, nothing.*

Fear began to prick at me when anyone else took Toby outside. I couldn't bear to look at the gap between the floats. I wanted to shadow every person who took her in their arms, watching to make sure they held her tightly enough. Don't let *anything* get your child, my shadow self whispered.

As if it were my duty, I began to visit the dark water in my mind's eye every night before going to sleep. By coming to terms with its potential, I reasoned, I could ward off the darkness. The water, like the evil eye, could strike me if I wasn't paying attention. I kept my nocturnal visits secret and saw them as a way of fabricating a charm—a protective amulet to guard against the dark water. I hid my fear from everyone. But it guided my actions, tainted my thoughts. One day, I woke to a morning of perfection, the rising breath of the water shot through with sunlight. From my upstairs window, I saw a troupe of river otters swimming underwater, bubbles streaming in their wake. As their supple bodies arrowed past, I sighed, wanting to share the moment with Toby. But I didn't want to take her near the water's edge because... because.... With sudden clarity, I saw the trap I was falling into. Fear was coming first. Toby didn't see otters that morning, but I promised she would see them the next time. Somewhere between the dark water and the bright water, there had to lie a balance.

Part of growing up is knowing where home is. But the floathouse was a limited environment. I wanted Toby's sense of home to be broader, inclusive of inlets and mountains and stars and people and history. As winter fell away, I began to show her what home meant, one outing at a time.

Boating with a baby is an awkward activity. First there are infant life jackets, never a popular item. Then there are hands; I needed four, but only had two. Landing on shore includes throwing anchor, lifting the motor and tying shore lines. If the tide is ebbing, it's important to prevent the boat from getting stranded. All of these things are formulaic, but babies are known for their ability to disrupt even the best-planned events. I dusted off the baby backpack we'd been given and tried to simplify my system of anchoring.

Marcel's work as a diver and boat driver meant that he was often unreachable by cellphone in the event of an emergency. For that reason, our mother-daughter boating outings started small. At high tide we went to Aquila Island, adjacent to the floathouse, to admire the lush forest and point out specifics (ferns, lichen, cedar bark).

Soon after, we went to Meares Island, boating to Ginnard Creek waterfall where it cascades into the inlet (splish-splash!). And once Toby was able to sit up, we began to visit a small islet we called Cathie's rock. The grassy knoll on Cathie's rock was a vantage point from which to see our world (home, channel, island). But the islet offered something else, an eagle feather dangling from a weathered tripod of sticks. The feather was important, the part of learning that included people and history.

Before I lived in Maltby Slough, the bay was home to Mike and Cathie and their daughter, April. They were role models to me in the ways of wilderness living. Quiet and determined, Cathie insisted on living by example: appreciating nature, living humbly, leaving no trace. But when April was ten, Cathie began treatment for leukemia. And before April was twelve, Cathie died. For some time we'd been communicating only by letter, as her strength ebbed. Her love of nature sustained her and she wrote of spring sweeping over the mudflats, the blossoming of salmonberry flowers and the arrival of rufous hummingbirds. She'd begun to meditate, hanging an eagle feather at a small grassy island. I liked to picture her there, even though she was less and less able to leave the house.

Cathie's life ended in the spring, several years before I moved to Maltby Slough. I was sweeping the floor of the Stone Island cabin when I was overcome by a feeling of certainty that she had died. I stood in the middle of the room next to my dust pile, staring out of the window at the water as sadness washed over me. But I wasn't yet a parent. I saw death only from the viewpoint of those left behind.

I took Toby to Cathie's rock one windy spring day when she was seven months old. She was at the age of sitting up and reaching forward, almost crawling. It was finally spring, clear and sunny, but with a gale force northwester galloping across the blue sky. At winter's end, being indoors is akin to being underground, the body craving escape from dankness and confinement, the mind dreaming of light and air. Up in the canopy, branches bent low and the wind breathed in monophonic plainsong, punctuated by sudden sustained crescendos. The floathouse shifted and tugged on its mooring lines and I didn't have to be in Browning Passage to picture the expanse of frothing whitecaps I would see there. Of my options, Cathie's rock seemed the safest bet for an outing. I pulled out warm clothes, a blanket and a thermos. I put on our life jackets and wrestled Toby into the baby backpack before pulling it onto my shoulders. As a precaution against drowning I left the hip belt and Toby's shoulder straps unfastened. Then I pulled the door closed and got into the boat.

We approached the lee of the island on water that was mostly calm, but occasionally feathered by gusts. The tide was flooding, so I didn't need a stern anchor. A tumble of rocks made an intertidal stairway of sorts. It also provided plenty of nooks in which to lodge my makeshift shore anchor—a perfectly round, fifteen-pound lead

weight. A shore anchor needs to be easy to throw, something you can chuck first, then use for pulling the boat to land. This lead fishing weight worked well for me—heavy enough to stay where it landed, but not so heavy that I couldn't throw it a few metres.

In the backpack, excitement was running high. Loud squeaks vied with the noise of motor and wind. A fist was wrapped around my ponytail and two plump legs flailed against my back. I lifted the motor, then sat on the bow, pulling on the shore anchor to bring the boat closer to land. In the slippery intertidal, I struggled to keep my footing under the top-heavy load. I picked my way up the rocks, arms out for balance, examining the placement of the anchor. With an incoming tide, I didn't have to worry about the boat being stranded, but I needed to move the lead weight higher, above tide's reach. I tugged on the weight. In the way of such things, it rolled deeper into the crevice. I tugged harder, leaning sideways to change the angle of pull. The backpack slid sideways too, threatening to disgorge its contents. Squeaks became squawks, and the beginnings of a wail rang out over my head. I shrugged the load back into position and began a chorus of "This Little Pig" as I heaved on the rope, dislodging the anchor and stumbling as it came free. Another wail began, the rapidly ascending note of which inspired a great sense of urgency in me. Hefting the lead weight, I threw it uphill

with a grunt, gave the line a quick tug and climbed the rocks with as much velocity as I could muster. On the grassy knoll, I jogged here and there, cavorting until the wails subsided and—crisis averted—it seemed safe to sit down.

We sat in the lee of some huckleberry bushes and enjoyed the sun, the mossy grass and an early, exuberant hummingbird. The needs of infants are capricious and hard to identify, both for the baby and the parent. Seven months into parenthood my learning curve was still steep. Using Toby's facial expressions as my guide, we swung between snuggling, singing and playing peekaboo with the blanket. Our life jackets made a corral of sorts, protecting against sharp rocks and the sudden downward slope of the knoll. Out on the water, brushstrokes of wind painted the surface with swaths of shadow, evaporating with the passage of each gust. From time to time a passing gust would be inspired to tear at my hair, but mostly we were sheltered, soaking up the sun. I scanned the landscape for signs of wolves and wondered, as always, about cougars. Might predators be attracted to the plentiful mice, whose tunnels criss-crossed the grass in every direction? Might a predator have walked here at low tide and still be concealed in the trees? It was hard to look at my bite-sized child and not feel the need to remove every hazard. As my attention vacillated between peekaboo and scouting, I imagined my mother with me at this stage. In Trinidad, the dangers were smaller—scorpions, centipedes, snakes— but just as potentially fatal, if not more so. My mother now lived in England, where she and Toby had met, recently, for the first time. I'd been touched by the dimensions a child could add to a relationship: the sudden sense of connection that comes with the revolving generational wheel.

A gust of wind whipped my hair, interrupting my musings. And a clunking sound caught my attention. I sat up, wondering at the source of the sound. When I heard it again, I ran to the edge of the slope, just in time to see my boat being pushed by the force of a gust

and my lead ball anchor, the source of earlier troubles, being pulled down the rocks, into the water—splish-splash!

I ran toward the boat. It was drifting—anchor and all. But a wail from the blanket tugged me to a standstill. Where before I would have leaped down the rocks and swum out to the boat, now I hesitated, glancing back at the hilltop rising up between my child and me. I scanned again for danger, even though the real danger lay in losing the boat. But as if restrained by a magnetic field, I found I couldn't move forward. Precious seconds evaporated. I wanted to go after the boat, but I couldn't leave my baby. Those seconds were all it took for the boat to drift too far away, the lead ball bouncing along the soft mudflat. I closed my eyes. Defeat rang in my ears. Seven months in and already I'd failed in my duty to keep us safe. It was windy! We shouldn't have come! I was careless with anchoring because it was difficult with Toby in the backpack. And now we were marooned. And what was going to happen to my boat? What had I been *thinking*?

I ran back up the hill, wondering what I would see. Might Toby have fallen over? Might she have somehow crawled forwards, inching toward the steep rocky slope? Would I arrive in time to avert a disaster? I held my breath, but when she came into view she was smiling and waving. I waved back at her, exhaling with relief. She wasn't waving at me, though. Her gaze was drawn elsewhere. I turned to find out who she was looking at and saw that she wasn't waving hello at all, she was waving bye-bye—waving bye-bye to the boat. I collapsed onto the blanket, laughing and pulling her into my arms. We always waved goodbye to Marcel's boat when he left in the mornings, but we did it together. Now, she was (literally) taking matters into her own hands. We sat in the grass in the sun, watching the boat grow smaller and further away, in thrall to the joy of waving. I guessed the boat would continue drifting north past the house, past the island and out toward open water. There it would be exposed to the full force of the northwester and be pushed across the mudflats to some shallow and muddy place where it would be annoyingly difficult to retrieve. Powerless to change anything, I had to stop fretting. Marcel would come home eventually. We would hear the roar of his boat motor as he came into the bay and could surely hail him from the island.

While the boat blew away from us, Toby and I explored the island further, ending up at the eagle feather. The simple sticks had weathered to grey and the feather was stripped of lustre by the unstoppable winter winds. But even so, as it bobbed and turned in the air, it captured our full attention—Toby reaching out to it with both hands, while I put my thoughts of the drifting boat on pause. Before having a baby, when I'd come to visit the feather, I'd dedicated myself to thoughts of Cathie. I remembered her observations of nature and shared my own. I pictured her shy smile and told her I missed her.

But sitting there with a baby in my lap I saw a new and bitter sorrow in Cathie's death, that of a mother parting from her child. The fluttering feather spoke of impermanence, the lack of certainty in life. I was pierced by the reality of leaving behind a child, the unfinished business of parenting. With time, even the best memories fade. What if my child went through life not knowing how greatly I loved her? I tightened my hold on Toby and thought about my father's death five years earlier. His importance to me was something I could only tell her about, nothing she could feel or know for herself. What if I, like Cathie, had to rely on someone else to tell Toby about me? Would I like their choice of words? Would they remember my successes without mentioning my failures? What if they described me only as a writer? What about all the other parts of me? The concept of letting go seemed exquisitely painful once a child was involved.

I wondered, suddenly, about my own mother. She didn't speak about herself much. Did I know enough about her? I knew that when I was two, she went alone into the Pacaraima Mountains of Guyana. A missionary walked her to the remote Amerindian village of Kurukubaru and left her there, returning for her three weeks later. Her paintings from that time in Guyana are of cloud-shadowed blue hillscapes, women, children and scenes of Amerindian village life. The paintings convey her love of landscape and interest in people, but they don't tell the story of a woman torn between art and adventure on one hand, and a brood of five children on the other. I imagine the emancipation she must have felt while painting—the hunger to make up for lost time. How many other stories was I missing out on? How lacking was my sense of her? As my mother aged, now entering her eighties, the unique and wild experiences of her life were coalescing, gathering into an essence she would take with her when she died.

Children and adventure. My attention wavered and I couldn't help scanning for the boat. I looked up as it was passing the floathouse. Any minute now it would drift around the corner and be lost from sight…. I felt myself pulled to action, but the feather fluttered, reminding me to let go. I thought again of my mother, of the memories she would take with her and those she would leave behind. Thoughts and memories are unique to each individual, only becoming mutual where they intersect with those of others. Perhaps explanations weren't needed, after all. Being stranded at Cathie's rock showed Toby a choice I'd taken: for safety's sake, we could have stayed at home; for the love of the outdoors, we'd taken a risk, one that I hoped would end well. How would this reflect on me? Any conclusions she would draw would be her own—more meaningful for being so. A parent can't change those perceptions; it would be disingenuous to try. For the rest, holding Toby on my lap, I felt the fierce, universal love that comes with bearing a child. If her future held the happenstance of parenthood, she wouldn't need anyone else to tell her how I felt. She would know.

We'd been gazing at the feather for some time when a strange thing happened. The boat had drifted down the channel past the floathouse. But at a distance of about five hundred metres it was caught by counter-gusts coming from Browning Passage. It began to be pushed southwest. Surprised, I charted the course it was taking—a wide circle that seemed, incredibly, to lead right back to Cathie's rock.

We sat on the knoll to watch the boat's progress. At two hundred metres, Toby began waving—this time hello. I held my breath. At twenty metres, Toby was ecstatic, waving and burbling with glee. Daring to hope for the best, I put our life jackets on and put Toby in the backpack. At five metres I waded out barelegged to the boat. I threw my boots and pants on board and swung the backpack over the gunwales, putting Toby down in the boat. I climbed aboard, pulling up the wayward shore anchor, and within a few minutes we were motoring. We neared the floathouse in full voice (this little pig went wee wee wee all the way home!) just as Marcel's boat came around the point.

I'll never know the combination of wind and current that took my boat away and brought it back. Things like that just happen out here, part of the magic. And included in the magic was a lesson I needed to learn. When I first saw that little hand waving, I was chanting self-chastisements. But when I realized what Toby was doing, the stress fell away and I was able to enjoy her delight. And I saw that what I should fear, more than the dark water, was destroying a child's delight. It's children who remind us how to find joy in simple things. And if we can't encourage joy in children, we become, simply, keepers.

I want my daughter to share my love for the water and the wild. But the wild has dangers, as does civilization, as does life. I have to show her the beauty and the danger; guard her without seeming to guard her; watch the dark water in private. I have to be honest about my fears without burdening her with the guilt of them. It's been done by my mother before me, and it has been done by mothers through the ages. I've even done it myself, on a windy, blue-skied day at Cathie's rock, where—at that moment in time—a wind-stripped feather, a vanishing boat and a waving child taught me so much about letting go.

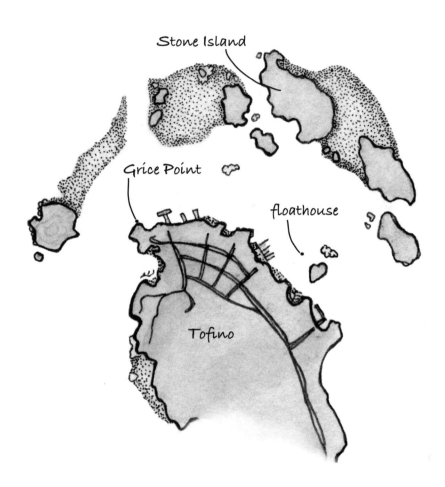

Stone Island

Grice Point

floathouse

Tofino

this land emerging
from mist; ravens, bears, clamshells
stories—found and lost

Say the Names

I'm not good at names, or bad at them. I haven't gone through life stuffing my quiver with an arsenal of names. I remember people's essence—hare-brained, hair-trigger, loving, serious. I remember people because I've worked with them or shared food with them. I always remember if I've joked with them. And sometimes a name seems special, or relevant. But I never expected a name to save my life.

On a late-summer evening, fourteen years after moving to Tofino, I tucked my toddler daughter into bed and set out on a sunset paddle. By then Marcel and I had moved the floathouse back to the Tofino Harbour from Maltby Slough. The evening was perfect, the water glassy and the sky gathering colour with every minute. I caught the ebbing tide, whooshing away from the floathouse with a satisfying flourish. Nearing the cormorant rocks in the middle of the harbour, a boat passed me, heading to the village of Opitsaht. I waved, recognizing the passengers. When they didn't wave back, I took off my paddling hat and sunglasses and waved again. This time I was identified and given a wave in return. When I was in my motorboat people knew me instantly, so it irked me to go unrecognized when I was in my kayak. Kayaking was my life—know me, know my kayak. I had to remember that it was also, to some, a mild form of eccentricity, regarded with gentle puzzlement: why paddle when you can drive? Many boaters can't tell one kayak from another and in the marine community kayaks are known, somewhat predictably, as speed bumps. It didn't matter to me if people knew my name, but I did want them to know that I wasn't just a stranger, or a speed bump, that the kayaker was me.

But in some ways I was accustomed to being unrecognized. In the summer of 1990, when I first arrived in Tofino, I met Carl, the Tla-o-qui-aht man who would become my partner for the next seven years. And as we got to know each other better, he introduced me to his family. Arriving by boat at the village of Opitsaht, I was often swarmed by giggling troupes of children calling out: "What is your name? Why are you here?" And no matter how many times I stopped to say hello, say my name, say who I was visiting, I was still often greeted this way, year after year.

Those years were an education. When I'd arrived in Canada three years earlier, my notion of First Nations people was limited to the carvings of Bill Reid and the contents of the Museum of Anthropology at the University of British Columbia. I had no context for an actual living, breathing, present-day culture.

But 1990 gave me a crash course.

Night after night I lay awake, examining the slant of my partner's cheekbones and the heaviness of his long black hair. In a state of mild culture shock, I wondered who I was and how we had come to be together. By contrast, my partner had a strongly defined sense of self. A proud canoe carver and charter boat operator from a large family, he knew what he stood for and what he wouldn't stand for. He told me of injustices endured by First Nations people at the hands of European settlers and church representatives. I learned how this injustice had carried through to the present day.

That was the summer of the Oka crisis. Even without my new perspective on life, the notion of building a golf course on a burial ground seemed deliberately provocative. *Golf*, of all frivolous things! Ancestral remains were an issue in Clayoquot Sound, too. Burial caves had been looted by non-Native old-timers, claiming an interest in history. Burial islands had become the domain of summer homes, small cabins cropping up amid the ancient spruce trees, in whose high branches were lodged the remains of ancestors, preserved in moss-draped wooden boxes.

Tofino at the time was a hot-button place, having lived through the heated environmental protests of Meares Island and Sulphur Passage. The logging of Meares Island was prevented through a concerted effort by First Nations people and environmentalists, thus in many ways these two groups—with a mixed array of aims, from preservation to land rights—wound up on one side of a fence, while the logging fraternity squared up along the other.

Add to this restless mix a long history of Saturday night fights between Natives and non-Natives outside the Maquinna bar and you have the basis for the kind of explosive behaviour of September 8, 1990, at the intersection of First and Campbell streets in Tofino.

On that day in September, what started out as an information protest about the army at Oka, and the stoning of Mohawk women and children there, erupted into a geyser of aggression. The protest was planned as a peaceful affair but turned into a volatile mess of beer-drinking hecklers shouting racist epithets, and hyper-charged people in trucks trying to ram the protestors, about 75 percent of whom were non-Native. Two children narrowly escaped being run over. Innocent tourists were threatened. Communication was reduced to "Fuck you, fucking asshole!" Even Old Ben, one of my favourite Elders, is forever etched in my mind's eye, waving his stick above his head and yelling to the hecklers in his frail voice, "Why don't you come over here and tell me that?"

What shocked me was the rapidity with which the situation ignited. My small town had flown from peace to war in five minutes. The aggression was supported by a self-righteous anger that had no clear foundation and yet it was there, simmering under the surface in a way I hadn't perceived. I saw with sudden clarity what my partner meant when he told of the prejudice he and his family had faced in their lives. And the words of Hesquiaht chief Simon Lucas—who had spoken beautifully at the close of the protest—echoed through my head:

"You only see us with one eye."

Following that summer, we settled into a shared life. Our small apartment filled with things my partner and I had made together—a table, shelves, small carvings. I drove the boat and helped with the winter beachcombing of logs. I dug clams, picked oysters, ate duck soup, fish-head soup, herring roe and many other traditional foods. I began to learn Tla-o-qui-aht words, kept a dictionary, listened to the soft nuances of the language.

At around this time I was reading *The Songlines*, by Bruce Chatwin. In it, he told of Australian aborigines, for whom the world is not alive until they have walked through time—along dream tracks dating back to creation—singing each landmark into existence along the way. I identified with the aborigines. I, too, was awakening to a new world, its features coming alive for me as I did so.

I attended potlatches and regular family dinners. Slowly, I began to meet the large group of people who made up my new family. And without exception they were friendly, welcoming, kind. When spring arrived I felt like a changed person. But who was I? I didn't know yet.

And then I experienced a different kind of baptism.

When they came, the deaths were brutal, shocking, relentless. My partner's beautiful eleven-year-old niece died in a tragic accident. Until that moment, my exposure to death included the natural demise of an elderly grandmother and a high-school acquaintance killed in a car crash. I grappled with the split-second ending of this young life, wondering how my partner's sister could ever survive the loss of a child. It didn't seem possible that her daughter, so young and lively, was dead.

My dreams changed, becoming troubled. One morning I awoke to an image of slaughter, a heap of animals dead on the rocks at an island. What woke me was the phone ringing. Another message of death—this time the death of a nephew. Again, I failed to make sense of it. This young man had just graduated high school, voted most popular student. This young man, whose life was just taking flight, had deliberately planned its end.

And then there was another nephew, this one killed in a conflict. I hadn't been prepared for another death, so soon and so violent. I felt reborn, but not in the positive sense of that phrase. For me, the passage was from light into darkness, the darkness of things that shouldn't be. If I had been searching for a song-line, by now it could be the comfort of Mozart's powerful *Requiem*.

By this time I had also learned that grief could be a community affair. No hushed whispers or darkened doors. No leaving people alone or giving them space for reasons of privacy. Here, one's presence in a grieving household was considered a mark of utmost respect. Human company was known to be the best possible medicine. Visitors came from all over to sit with the grievers in living rooms packed with rows of chairs.

I became proficient in the culture of death, the protocols required. When word of a death reached our ears, we went to the Co-op and filled bags with essentials: coffee, bread, cheese, ham and mayonnaise. Hundreds of people would pass through the grieving household, requiring nourishment. And then there were the coffins. For a family facing an unexpected death, or several deaths in a row, the cost of a coffin is crippling. Even in winter, when work was scarce, we would empty our pockets and hand over what we had: crumpled fives, tens—

sometimes even coins. Rent seemed trivial compared with the need for a coffin. Time, also, seemed irrelevant on these occasions. One's own plans became unimportant, replaced by the need to help wash dishes, pass out food, or simply sit in silent solidarity with the gathered crowd.

The deaths continued apace. A rash of suicides culminated with that of an eight-year-old boy. In what was another first for me, a young man died of AIDS. A young woman vanished without a trace, last seen at a party, still lost even now.

I began to see my new community as a people in perpetual crisis. There never seemed to be time to heal from one event before the next one struck. The paralysis of grief affected everyone. Death cast long shadows, in the darkness of which it was impossible to function. By comparison, John Jewitt, a blacksmith from the ship *Boston* who had been a slave of the Mowachaht tribe two hundred years prior, remarked on the robust health of the people, their strength, toughness, and the astonishing paucity of deaths. In the three years that he spent with them, from 1803 to 1805, only five people died out of fifteen hundred. I read his diary with a bitter sense of wonder. So much had changed.

While I was stuck in my newfound state of bewilderment, Tofino was also changing. In 1993 close to a thousand people were arrested in defense of Clayoquot Sound. Multinational logging corporation MacMillan Bloedel fell to its knees, while tourists from around the world arrived to see the place that had achieved such international media attention. By now, I saw the world with a built-in set of contrasts—the world I'd grown up in and the world I was only just beginning to know. I also saw two communities rapidly diverging.

Tourism spawned a housing boom in Tofino. In the equivalent of an old-fashioned gold rush, land mongers, developers and speculators rushed onto the peninsula. Land was no longer a place of story and connection. Many buyers were strangers, separated from our small community by their wealth and newness. By contrast, the Native community, so entrenched in family and historical connection, was collecting for coffins. The cultural divide was already conspicuous. The wealth gap was making it more so—resentment in the making. Taking a minor key, my song became one of unease. What did the future hold?

Carl and I separated after seven life-changing years. His own life continued to be wracked by tragedy—the loss of a grandson, the loss of a daughter, the loss of his father. With his father went the family home and I no longer had a place to visit in Opitsaht. Deprived of my usual way into the community, I felt shy, uncertain how to proceed. I also realized that my honest, funny and curious Opitsaht welcome of "What is your name? Why are you here?" was what many Tla-o-qui-aht people felt every day in Tofino, minus the elements of honest, funny or curious. For them, the element is invisibility, or worse, hostility. And one day I learned how that felt.

It was now 2006. Stage after stage, my life had been changing. I'd spent several years living alone on a floathouse in a remote bay; met and joined households with Marcel, a man who also lived afloat; become pregnant; had a child; and eventually come full circle, mooring the floathouse back in the Tofino Harbour at the same dock where I first started out. As with all new parents, free time was precious, packed with things that needed to be done. But on that beautiful evening I had only one thing to do: enjoy the moment.

Gliding out of the harbour on the ebbing tide, I passed close to Grice Point, the sheer rock bluff where tides are measured. Twenty feet up on the bluff a group of Native boys was partying. I could tell by their whooping cries that they were high—very high. They noticed my kayak and made a joke. Then they guffawed and came to the edge of the bluff, looking down at me, still laughing.

"Throw the rock," one shouted. And quick as winking, the second boy hefted a boulder into his arms, grunting at the effort. The third boy hung back.

So close to the bluff, I was an unmissable target. The rock just had to be dropped and it would strike either my boat or myself. If it hit me, my skull would not survive the impact. If the rock hit the kayak, it would destroy the deck, capsize and sink the boat. I began to sweat, tightening my grip on the paddle. Fear for my daughter swirled with the eddies. Those volatile seconds had the power to change her life, too. To the boys on the bluff, I was a faceless kayaker, just as they—daily—were faceless to non-Native people in Tofino. Two communities living side by side, unknown to each other. But there was a difference here. I wasn't just a kayaker, or a speed bump. I was a person and I knew these boys. They'd been children when I first moved to Opitsaht, bright laughing faces greeting me at the dock or on the road. My voice carried strongly up the bluff as I greeted one of the boys by his name. There was a silent pause and the other boys turned to him.

"How come she knows your name?"

I never heard the reply because they moved away from the edge. Instead, I heard the dull thud of the rock as it fell to the ground—dropped, not thrown.

For the Australian aborigines, a *tjuringa* is a sacred stone, engraved with the part of a song-line that belongs to you. In recent years I've retraced the steps of my song-line, going backwards to find my way forward. I haven't yet found the perfect words to engrave, but what stands out is the importance of names. Names are the only way we have of showing recognition. It is difficult to crush someone with a rock if you know their name. Likewise, it is harder to diminish people—treat them as lesser or treat them with disrespect—if you know their name, their circumstances, their lovable traits, their weaknesses.

If cultures are to cross the gulf that separates them, in Tofino and elsewhere, it may be best to begin with individual relationships, the recognition of people as people. And as we say each other's names, so we sing them alive, awakening our own selves along the way.

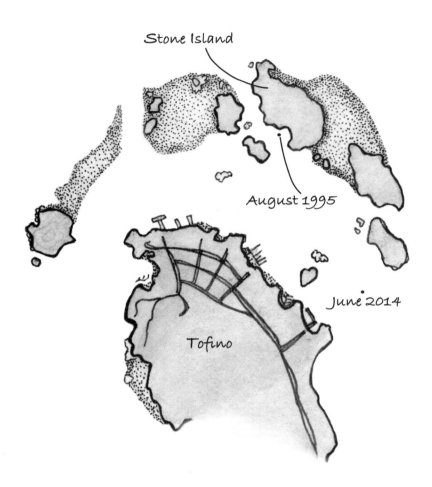

sculpted by the tide,
the waves, the wind. Perfection
at the water's edge

Finders Keepers

The most precious thing I ever found was a small green Japanese fishing float. This glass ball had escaped its net in a storm and drifted thousands of miles, washing up at my feet at Wickaninnish Beach, on Vancouver Island's west coast, in 1990. It was about the size of a tennis ball and I'd been searching for it for months. In those days I worked at the Wickaninnish Interpretive Centre on Long Beach. Every lunch break, heavy winter rains notwithstanding, I'd scour the beach in hope of finding what is surely the beachcomber's most coveted treasure. But I'd always understood that a glass ball's story would end once it was found. I didn't expect that my future life on the water would enable the story to continue.

Living on water has many perks: light from the water's surface dappling the ceiling; the hypnotic glide of the current; the wildlife—seals, birds, whales—passing without warning; and the way the landscape transforms from land to water to land again. Once, after I'd been living on the water for several years, I visited my family in England and experienced a strange variant of culture shock. No matter how often I went to the window, the green lawn never once crept closer or retreated. The view never changed, though I had.

But there are drawbacks to living on the water. There are the storms: tedious insomnia from listening to the house creak and groan; the jarring tug of the lines as gusts of wind push the house to its point of maximum resistance; the daily commutes made complicated by wind and waves. And there are the little things: the maintenance of boats and motors; the impossibility of walking anywhere without taking a boat first; the sulphurous mats of summer seaweed; the maintenance of anchor lines; the falling in of people, dogs, objects—keys, sunglasses, cellphones, hammers, nails, pieces of firewood—the list is long. Some things are recoverable. Act quickly and you can get them back. Others sink, disappearing into soft dark mud, an Atlantis of lost items, the ocean floor littered with strange clues.

Sinking problems aside, the movement of floating objects by water has a mythical attractiveness few can resist. Ocean charts show swirling currents, tiny arrows leading from here to there, continent to continent, culture to culture. Occasionally the arrows culminate in a gyre from which some objects never escape, or sailors arrive in horse latitudes where they languish, becalmed, for days on end. The shoreline, too, is a provider of surprises. Beachcombing is a much-loved pastime, casual for some, obsessive for others. But the finding of objects is based on the premise that the objects have first been removed from somewhere else. One woman's gift is another woman's loss.

I knew about glass balls because my father had found them when I was a child growing up in the West Indies. He'd been lucky enough to find a large one, turquoise-green, about the size of a beach ball. On the day I found mine, I was particularly pleased because a well-known glass ball fanatic had been on the beach not long before me. The ball had somehow escaped detection by his experienced eyes, so it felt as if this treasure was truly meant for me.

After so many months, when I finally saw the small green shape glistening on the sand, I stared for several long seconds, belief suspended. Then I pounced on it. I clutched it to my chest. I whooped. A pair of ravens eyed me askance and hop-waddled to the safety of the driftwood logs. I ran the length of the beach, laughing.

For days afterwards, the story of this precious treasure echoed through my head as I re-enacted the moment for friends and family members—or to anyone who would listen. And there it sat, on my counter, prompting me to recall its moment of discovery every time I saw it. I admired the way it glowed in the light of a candle—the captured breath of the glass blower brought alive by the flame. I thought of that breath, the way a single exhalation had kept the glass afloat through years of work and further years of travel, as it crossed the vast Pacific. As glass balls go, it may have been small and ordinary, but to me it was extraordinary.

In 1995, five years after finding the glass ball, I moved from the cabin on Stone Island in the Tofino Harbour, down the ramp to my freshly constructed floathouse, moored at the same island's dock. Friends came over to move boxes down the long pier that stretched high over the water before descending a precarious ramp to the floathouse. This moving party was a celebration. After years of do-it-yourself carpentry, no part of which is ever simple on a floathouse, and for which I have little aptitude anyway, there was now a finished product and I had become a homeowner. Finally, I could unpack the boxes of belongings I hadn't seen for years. But all of this was happening at the busiest time of year for a sea kayak guide. I was working long days, often getting home at dark. So while the moving of the boxes was significant, unpacking would have to wait. About a week later, one of the helpers remembered something that had happened during the move and thought to tell me about it. "By the way," he said, "while we were moving stuff, one of your glass balls rolled out of a box. It landed in the water and floated away."

I sat down.

"*One* of my glass balls?" I echoed, grasping the back of the chair for support.

"You know," he continued, waving his hand, "one of those little green ones."

"Oh," I said, trying to keep my face from collapsing. "One of those."

I mourned my glass ball. I pictured its moment of loss: the long sloping pier, twenty feet above water in places. I saw the cardboard box, sandwiched between muscular forearms and sternum, its contents shifting with every footfall. I saw the gaps between the weathered planks, the deep green water glinting. I saw the downward migration of the box, from sternum to abdomen, forcing the carrier to stop at the railing and reposition. I pictured arms thrusting the box upward to renew their grasp. And there it was—the small green glass ball sailing out over the worn wooden railing, falling so lightly, just the merest splash.

One woman's loss.

Did it go back out to sea? Or did it wash up at my neighbour's place, the next island in the harbour? Was it worthwhile to search for it, or would that be futile? I studied the chart and checked the tides for the date and time it had floated away. My heart sank when I saw that the tide had been ebbing strongly. With a despondent finger, I traced the line of the outgoing current. My glass ball had an unimpeded passage straight out to sea.

It was a lesson in letting go, although I didn't have a choice. In a half-hearted way, I hoped that whoever found my glass ball would whoop with joy as I had done and set it in pride of place on their shelf. In a secret way, I hoped that the ball was lodged nearby, in a swirling back-eddy of seaweed perhaps, and—in the ultimate too-good-to-be-true scenario—that I would see it from my kayak one day as I guided tourists around the harbour. This shred of optimism, I later learned, is what keeps glass ball collectors searching, day after stormy day. Even though I knew it was silly, I struggled to fully accept the loss. But my losses were not over. In the graph of life lessons, Possession and Loss zigzag across my timeline in giant steps.

The following winter, my place of work took delivery of an order of puppets. Some of them were furry animals, but the finger puppets that caught my eye were the funny little witches, with fuzzy hair, squinty eyes and red-and-black striped stockings. Since I was at a loss for gifts to send home, I thought that maybe my three sisters would get a laugh out of these *toil-and-trouble* puppets, just as I had done.

On a Friday afternoon at the post office I filled out the airmail forms, ticked the box that said "gift" and giggled out loud when I noted the contents: witches—3. This was at a time when there were still heated battles over the fate of Clayoquot Sound, and for some old-timers, the surging wave of Earth warriors, hippie activists and non-violent Wiccan eco-feminists was a source of great distress. So I wasn't the only one who took note of the word "witches" written on my form. The post-mistress also noticed—narrowing her eyes and pursing her lips. Funnily enough, this later turned out to be useful. I spent the weekend writing last-minute Christmas cards and returned to the post office on a Monday to send them. That was when the post-mistress took me aside and, with an air of great importance and conspiracy, whispered loudly that my parcel had been *stolen*. The story unfolded behind the back of her hand, for all to hear. The post office had been broken into over the weekend. The thieves made off with dozens of packages, but the job had been botched and the theft was discovered early. In a panic, the thieves ran down Neill Street, through a little-known trail to a rocky bay, spilling parcels as they went. By flashlight, they ripped open the parcels, seeking anything of value. They took what they could before red and blue lights began flashing and they stashed the rest of the booty, planning to return when the coast was clear. Their trail was too obvious and their route was discovered, along with part of their stash. But the thieves were landlubbers and had not taken into account the rising tide. My parcel, "the one with the *witches*," the post-mistress hissed in a significant voice, had floated away on the tide.

For most people, this problem would be easily surmountable. But in my family, I am the person who is always late; I am the "dog-ate-my-homework" sibling. With the witches safely mailed, this was going to be one of the first Christmases ever that my presents stood a chance of arriving on time. Now broke and out of gift ideas, I called home, my heart sinking. No one said they didn't believe me, but I had to wonder. Given my track record, would *I* have believed me?

Over the next few days, I chewed my nails and wondered what presents I could think up now. Tofino in those days was not a shopping Mecca. But as I was walking past the post office a few days later, the post-mistress rushed out to flag me down. Bouffant and beaming, she led me into the back of the building and there on the floor in a cardboard box were my witches. Two of them still had parts of the packaging attached. All of them were soaking wet—a tangle of eelgrass and hemlock needles, with a bit of sand thrown in.

"They washed up at Clayoquot Island," she gushed. "The caretakers found them this morning. They knew about the theft, so they brought them back. I didn't realize your witches were puppets!" she added. "They're really quite cute."

"But they can obviously do spells," I said, the width of her smile diminishing. "They wouldn't have survived otherwise, would they?"

I took the witches home and washed them, but they'd now taken on a battered appearance and I was never able to rid their fuzzy hair of hemlock needles. I dried them out over the woodstove, re-wrapped and repackaged them, and sent them airmail to England. By some miracle, they arrived in time for Christmas. Two of them still sit on a London shelf, proof that what the sea takes is sometimes returned, with a story included.

The incident with the witches refreshed the idea of finding my glass float. I felt so sure that it was nearby. I didn't go out of my way to seek it, but I had faith in the mysterious repeating patterns of the universe.

I scanned the shoreline wherever I went, always watching for that particular shape and colour. Several years later, my new partner, Marcel, found a glass ball similar to mine. I was happy to share his moment of triumph and knew how it felt. And the house felt better with his treasure in place. Sometimes, though, looking at his glass ball only reminded me of my own. Then in 2012, when our daughter was about seven years old, Marcel and I were coming back from signing tax returns in Ucluelet one March day when we decided to go for a good long walk on the beach. It was blowing southeast, gale force. I was in despair at the amount of tax owing, combined with the accountant's bill. When I saw debris scattered all over the beach, I said to Marcel, "Maybe I'll find a glass ball and that will make me feel better."

We walked for an hour in one direction, the rain driving into our faces and penetrating our supposed-to-be-waterproof raingear. There were several large black plastic floats on the beach, but no signs of glass balls: no Japanese light bulbs, no objects adorned with pelagic gooseneck barnacles, nothing to indicate that this would be a fruitful walk. We admired the shorebirds taking refuge from the storm, especially the elegant black-bellied plovers. We commented on how sodden we were as we turned around and began the hour-long walk back. And that was when I saw a spherical object that was not black, but green.

"Look there!" I said. "What's that?"

Marcel pulled out his binoculars and peered into the distance.

"It's a huge great glass ball, is what it is!" he yelled.

Gumboots, raingear and all, we ran, speeding up and panting with the effort as we saw two other walkers heading that way. The walkers apparently didn't know about glass balls, because they looked at us oddly and gave us a wide berth. But our run was worthwhile, because perched on the foam from a receding wave was a beach-ball-sized float. My household had grown to a family of three and the size of our find seemed to have grown along with us. The float's southern hemisphere was thickly clothed in green algae, but from its equator northward it gleamed of turquoise glass. Against the smoothness of glass were three lumpy Japanese "double F" insignias, trademarks of the Hokuyu Glass Company. These stamped insignias allowed us to pinpoint the float's origins, but they also increased the rarity of the find.

After this, I discovered just how fierce a competition I was up against. From out of the woodwork, people came up to me and asked about my glass ball. They wanted to know about the double F stamps; they wanted to know where I'd found it, what the weather had been doing that day—and the tide. In a subtle way, some people wanted to see if I understood or properly appreciated the value of my find. And then there were those who needed me to know that such a find was technically not something I deserved. These people had been combing the beaches every day before work, often going out in storms at four in the morning. The soles of their boots were caked with a winter's worth of sand, packed in tight, the accumulation of grains symbolic of their investment in the flotsam lottery. The more you have, the greater your chances? Not in this case. In this case, my presence on the beach in a storm was entirely random and the idea of looking for a glass ball was just as spontaneous. The fact that I'd happened to be in exactly the right place when the waves delivered their prize was pure chance. And for some people, this rankled. I was surprised to discover just how extensive this group of dedicated seekers was. In Tofino they communicate by text message, so that their early morning paths don't collide. They share information and keep secrets. They thirst for the sight of green glass on sand. They don't complain about the weather, or lack of sleep. Nor do young children slow them down. Infants and toddlers are strapped into backpacks, rain guards cinched tight, to join in the search. To say they are obsessed is close to the mark.

I was not obsessed about my lost float, but I had the restless feeling that I simply hadn't looked for it hard enough. I remember my father losing the car keys after a long workday in the Tobago bush. We returned to a locked car in blistering heat, miles from anywhere. I remember my brother and I edging into the deep green shade of a breadfruit tree as the *bloody hells* and *Jesus Christs* morphed into other words—words we weren't supposed to know, or hear. My father's face, already flushed from the heat, grew a deep shade of red and a perimeter of random objects grew around him, as he pelted them at the ground. When he threw his hat, the only thing left to throw, the keys tumbled from the top of his head. Their transition from invisible to visible made a big impression on me, so slight was the line between the two.

The new glass ball was not my little green float made visible. It was something else entirely. Finding it with Marcel meant that it belonged to *us*. In this way it mirrored the changes in my life—my expansion from individual to partner, and mother. Three stamps for our family of three. If the universe were sending me a message, the message seemed to be about living in the moment and appreciating what I had. I decided I should embrace the tale of the original float's loss and stamp it into my life story like a double F insignia. Surely, the story was as good as the object—perhaps better? And then I could just let it go…

This was when a new line arced across my graph of Possession and Loss.

Like the green Subaru owners that I began to notice and wave to once I owned a green Subaru myself, there was a group of people I was about to become affiliated with. Among this group were people who wanted something they couldn't have, struggled through their desires and made peace with their inability to achieve them. One friend finally came to terms with the idea that she might go through life childless. Two years later, she was married and had a child. Another friend finally gave up hoping she would ever have her writing published, changed professions, and the next year had a book on the shelves. There are more humble versions of this story, too. The gardener who nurtured a sickly plant for years, only to have a seedling spring up and flourish after the plant had died.

I didn't join this group until one June day in 2014. By then we had moved, mooring our home near Strawberry Island in the Tofino Harbour—the site of my first floathouse experience. Much had changed. Tofino was busier than ever. I yearned for the quiet calm of Maltby Slough and pined for my wild home. The house was rocked by continuous boat wakes and my ears rang with the roar of boats and planes. I lost faith in my ability to adapt and had to remind myself why we'd done so. The limits of an isolated floathouse were not healthy for everyone, especially not for a child so attracted to other children she'd once begun crawling across a road at the sight of them. But as winter came, the noise died down, whales and seals continued swimming past our moorage and even the short boat ride brought a connection to the water that helped me survive. Much of our view was spectacular—the mountains, glaciers and sandy beaches we couldn't see from Maltby Slough. And there were ways to keep a connection with wild places. We took to the rowboat, landing like castaways on unpeopled beaches.

On the day in question, I was in the rowboat with my daughter, going to visit friends on an island in the harbour. The day was sunny, the water was calm and the current was racing like a river along its prescribed path, peeling away from itself in whirlpool after whirlpool. Catching the current, we zoomed downstream, passing a number of spiralling back eddies. Foam and bubbles gathered at the centre of each eddy, indicating the power and energy of the tide. But one bubble, in one back eddy, was not white; it was green. In the space of time it took me to register that it could be a glass ball, the rowboat had been whisked far downstream. I heaved us around and brandished the oars at top speed, moving like a paddle wheeler against the current. I told my daughter that there was a funny-looking bubble I wanted to check out. I told myself that the bubble was a light bulb, a bottle, or truly just a bubble. Glass balls were never found in the harbour and they were seldom found floating. And it was June—long past glass ball season. My daughter, however, knew me well.

"Is it a glass ball?" she breathed.

"It could be," I admitted, digging in and yarding on the oars.

At that, she transformed into a nine-year-old charioteer: "Over there!" she shouted, "Faster, faster! I can see it! It's green! It's round!"

"It might be a light bulb," I panted as we crossed the eddy line, our hull spinning as the counter-current took hold of us. I drew in the oars, knelt and grasped a canoe paddle, reaching into the swirling nucleus of the current to pull us close to the round, green shape. The eddy swung us even closer until I could reach through the creamy bubbles and pull out a small glass float, just like the one I'd lost ten or more years before, though the chances of it being the same one were almost nil. I held it up for Toby to see, both of us giddy with elation. And as the sun glinted from the bright water, my focus drifted from her laughing face to the long, high pier of Stone Island, visible behind her, barely a kilometre away. The tide was racing past Stone Island, racing toward us as if making up for lost time.

I looked again at the glass ball in my hand. Moving back to the harbour had brought me full circle in more ways than one.

Epilogue

This collection has come to represent a time in my life that stood apart from the rest of it—an age, an era, a passage. Echachis, Stone Island and Maltby Slough became like time capsules that I could open if I wanted, but that rested firmly on the continuum of the past. Even as I felt these experiences falling away from me, a tide swept me onward, into the future.

At first I was hesitant to collect these stories. At the age of not-yet-fifty, who was I to write a memoir? But in this rapidly changing world, memoir is increasingly relevant. I realized this during the writing process, when trying to convey the experience of life before cellphones. Already, this reality has been forgotten by people of my age. And just as I can't conceive of a life without antibiotics, contraception or the right to vote, those younger than me simply cannot conceive of daily life unconnected to friends, answers, advice. In the short span of twenty years, much has changed. And because we forget so easily, we need to be reminded.

Change continues, sometimes for the better, sometimes for the worse, but stories help to review those changes and show the full range of human experience. For me, these stories act as an inner compass, staying my course in a changing world. They reiterate the importance to me of living simply, resisting society's lure of wealth and status, the need to keep a meaningful personal connection to the planet's vanishing refugia—the places that make real this wild, fierce thing we call life.

Acknowledgements

It's humbling to think of the people who have propped me up during the timeframe of this book. Foremost of these are Marcel and Toby, who have made me laugh, indulged my foibles, believed in my (invisible-until-published) work, shared a very small space with a writer and developed their own extra-sensory awareness of my deadlines.

Edye Geleynse is the wilderness dweller who inspired me to live on a floathouse. She made everything about floating seem easy, possible, normal and desirable. Mike Woods, Cathie Lebredt and April Robson also made me long to live afloat, as did Norma Baillie—a legendary west coaster, whose floating store in an isolated bay sold remarkable books and potato chips, both. Cindi Cowie never saw barriers to our shared wilderness adventures and put up with me during long hours in small storm-bound tents.

Joe Cousineau, Carl Martin, Ike Campbell, Shorty Hofman, Rod Palm and Marcel Theriault helped make this floathouse (or stop it from sinking). Many others have given their advice and time, all of which I am grateful for.

Janice Lore, Caroline Woodward and Cori Howard went above and beyond in sharing their time, friendship and invaluable literary wisdom, while Kathy Shaw, Nora Martin, Darryn Brown and Erin McMullan generously read and reacted to individual stories. Those dear friends on whose broad shoulders I have wept with writerly angst are Janice Lore, Darryn Brown, Jan Brubacher, Cori Howard and Marcel Theriault. Others who have been generous with their time and support are Dorothy Baert, Marion Syme and the many fine members of the Clayoquot Writers' Group.

Kathy Page, Caroline Woodward, Cori Howard and Adrienne Mason helped to demystify the workings of the publishing world, while John Barton, Danielle Metcalfe-Chenail and Shanna Baker were helpful in shaping previous iterations of these stories.

And then there is the terrific gang at Caitlin Press. Vici Johnstone is the fire juggler who took a chance on this collection. She's been a warm voice on the phone, guiding and overseeing all aspects of the whole. She placed extraordinary trust in my abilities and projected an unwavering belief in this book.

Working with an editor as wise and intuitive as Jane Silcott has been liberating. I've valued her sense of subtlety and rhythm, and her magpie eye for the glittering stuff of errors. The student in me hopes I'll be lucky enough to work with Jane again one day.

Lastly, the rest of the team at Caitlin have been professional, encouraging, efficient and a pleasure to connect with. I thank them for their attention to detail and genuine interest. They include Michael Despotovic, Ruth Daniell, Christine Savage and Patricia Wolf.

Thank you!

Notes

Some of these essays have seen the light of publication in previous years. They have since been adapted for this collection.

"The Brightness and Darkness of Lucifer" was published in the *Malahat Review*, 2016, and *Best Canadian Essays 2017* (Tightrope Books). It was also longlisted for the CBC Creative Nonfiction Prize, 2015.

Part of the essay "Scars" was published in *Hakai Magazine* under the title "Echoes of Lives Lost on Haida Gwaii." It has been blended with an earlier essay, "Finding Light in No-Man's Land," which was shortlisted for the Shiva Naipaul Memorial Prize for travel writing in *The Spectator* magazine, 2003.

"Radio Wave" first appeared in *Paddling Through Time*, published by Raincoast Books in 2002. It was later excerpted in *Shared Vision* magazine in 2001. *Wavelength* magazine published the original version of "The Colour of Time" in 2001, under the title "Rhapsody on a Theme of Ice," while "Fair Game" was one of my first dangerous moments. It began life as a cover story for *BBC Wildlife Magazine* in 2000, entitled "Wolf At My Door."

Cori Howard sought out my experience of motherhood on a floathouse for her collection, *Between Interruptions: 30 Women Tell the Truth About Motherhood*, published by Key Porter Books Ltd. in 2007. Pieces of that essay can be found in "Letting Go."

The original version of "Say The Names" was published in the anthology *In This Together: Fifteen Stories of Truth and Reconciliation*, edited by Danielle Metcalfe-Chenail (Brindle and Glass, 2016). At that time it was entitled "Dropped, Not Thrown." The new title is a tribute to my favourite Al Purdy poem—one I've read aloud at many events for its lyric beauty and vital sentiment. It can be found at: www.theglobeandmail.com/arts/say-the-names-by-al-purdy/article4161335, and/or *Beyond Remembering* by Harbour Publishing.